SCARED FEARLESS

Publication of this book was aided by a generous
gift from Nancy and Ted Paup.

SCARED FEARLESS

An Unlikely Agent in the US Secret Service

Kathryn Clark Childers

With Deborah Hickman Perry

Texas A&M University Press / College Station

This paper meets the requirements of ANSI/NISO Z39.48–1992
(Permanence of Paper).
Binding materials have been chosen for durability.

Library of Congress Control Number: 2021936479
Cloth: 978-1-62349-916-7
Ebook: 978-1-62349-917-4

For Cecil, my heart.

For Anna, my sister, my everything.
When I was born, she grabbed me up
like I was a doll under the Christmas tree,
and she has made me feel loved . . .
for the rest of my life.

Contents

Contents

Galleries of images follow pages 32, 73, 103, 121, 161, 177, and 196.

Foreword

IN 1970, I was deputy assistant director of protective forces for the United States Secret Service. At that time, we had over 1,100 male employees and no women. I had often thought that having female agents could be of tremendous benefit. Indeed, when I was the special agent in charge of First Lady Jacqueline Kennedy's detail from 1960 to 1964, there were many occasions when a woman on the protective detail would have been extremely helpful. But in this male-dominated organization, not everyone agreed. Fortunately, with the approval of Director James J. Rowley, we began exploring how to incorporate women into this 105-year-old agency.

The men in the Secret Service most often came with some law enforcement or military experience, but there were few women with those backgrounds. We decided to seek out highly motivated candidates that had other skills that we had learned over the years were useful for our protective and investigative missions. For instance, Mrs. Kennedy was an accomplished horsewoman, tennis player, and water skier. President Ford and his family, including daughter Susan, were expert downhill skiers. We needed agents with appropriate athletic skills to blend in with whatever activities our protectees were doing. Thus, we began searching for females in their early to midtwenties who were accomplished swimmers, experienced skiers, tennis players, or equestrians, and who had experience in the use of firearms. We realized it was going to be a challenge, but we began the search. The male-dominated Secret Service would be forever changed.

As deputy assistant director, I personally interviewed some of the original applicants, including Kathryn Clark. Although she had no military or law enforcement experience, she had an interesting background, a number of the skills we needed, and an attitude that made her a good candidate.

This book, *Scared Fearless*, is the story of how she became a Secret Service agent and the experiences she had on the job. Although I was a member of the headquarters staff when Kathy and the other four women were sworn in as agents, I must admit that I didn't fully recognize the challenges they faced. They were pioneers who blazed the trail for the hundreds of female agents that followed, and they continue to be essential to the Secret Service. Kathryn is an example as to why I am so proud of the females we employed and the tremendous value they added.

Clint Hill
Assistant Director
United States Secret Service (RET)

Acknowledgments

THANK YOU to the many souls who have impacted my life, given me a story to tell, and agreed to help me do it. Some I love, some I knew well, and some I didn't know at all.

A very special thank you to Phyllis, Sue Ann, Laurie, and Holly, who welcomed me into the fabled "First Five" detail. And, not to be forgotten, Denise, who was a good sport about being #6. They were cohorts in fighting crime, willing without reservation to protect and serve, comrades in arms and companions on the rocky path toward making women's history. We remain friends today. Someone once said, "Well behaved women rarely make history." Well, we were well behaved, and we did make history. We were also tough!

If I go back to the beginning of my journey I have to thank the times: the history, the politics, and the people who inhabited the earth in 1947. Luckily, I joined the march of the Baby Boomer generation and took the road less traveled.

Thank you to President John F. Kennedy for inspiring America to go the moon, "not because it was easy, but because it was hard." As a high school girl, I can remember that speech and believing it was my personal invitation to "Ask not what your country can do for you; ask what you can do for your country." "Imagine," I thought, "maybe he means girls too!"

Thank you to President Lyndon B. Johnson for the Civil Rights Act of 1964 and to President Richard Nixon for signing into law the opportunity for women to join federal law enforcement. Yes, the people and events playing out on the world stage impact each one of us more than you realize. I didn't know any of these men, but their decisions and actions changed the trajectory of my life forever.

Many women also helped changed the landscape that made my US Secret Service opportunity possible. Thank you to Annie Oakley and the women of the 1960s and '70s who took the bull by the horns and became the voice for women's rights—Supreme Court Justice Ruth Bader Ginsberg and Gloria Steinem, to name two—in addition to the thousands of women who marched and spoke up. Those times changed my life and became the basis of my story. How easily we forget!

Many would suggest women were leading the march in the midst of a women's revolution in 1970. Yet, it was a cadre of exceptional men who were willing to push the doors of opportunity open for women from the inside out—not always a popular position to take in the smoke-filled rooms of Washington DC. In my mind, the edict to give women an opportunity to serve in federal law enforcement can be traced to Secret Service Director James J. Rowley, Deputy Assistant Director Clint Hill, Assistant Director Jerry Parr, Washington Field Office Special Agent in Charge Charlie Gittens, and my personal "tough guys," Special Agents Angie Angelone and Mugsey O'Leary.

At the forefront, Clint Hill will forever be remembered as the courageous Secret Service agent who leapt onto the back of the presidential limousine in the midst of the assassination of President John F. Kennedy to protect First Lady Jacqueline Kennedy. He received the nation's highest civilian award for bravery and is a national hero. What people do not know is that Mr. Hill carried the torch for equal employment opportunities for women in the Secret Service. First, I believe he had confidence that bringing women on board would provide a resource that could enhance the agency's ability to carry out the mission. Secondly, Mr. Hill believed in us. He led the search for the right five for the initial test run. I will always be grateful I was chosen as one of them.

The same can be said for Jerry Parr, Charlie Gittens, and Angie Angelone, who always had my back. Their confidence trickled down through the ranks and convinced those who weren't so sure. Thank you to them and the men of the Secret Service who willingly joined in this grand experiment.

Historically, women's rights and opportunities have made great strides in the last 50 years. Many of the first steps taken in 1970 when the US Secret Service hired five girls in their 20's from across the country and got the ball rolling. And to the female agents who carried on and continue to do so today: thank you for proving that, when given the opportunity, women can be worthy of trust and confidence alongside men—or leading the way. We've earned it. Carry on, even if you need to do it scared.

Thanks to the interesting, famous, and important people I protected who believed my being in their shadow was worthy of trust and confidence—particularly former first lady Jacqueline Kennedy Onassis, Caroline Kennedy Schlossberg, and Princess Sofia of Spain.

Wrapping up the book, I was interested in knowing more about the Secret Service today. Thanks to US Secret Service Director of Communications Cathy L. Milhoan and her entire cracker jack staff in the Communications and Media Relations Division who invited me to visit headquarters in 2019. Meeting Assistant Director Leon Newsome in the museum where a photograph of the "First Five" is prominently displayed was gratifying. Yes, we are in the history books and even today the top brass seem proud of us. A special thanks to historian Mike Sampson who was willing to fill in the blanks and blow the dust of the records of the olden days, keeping me on track throughout this journey. And hats off to Starr Vazquez, who is a gal who can do anything! Taping a podcast with Cody Starken and former Special Agent Sue Ann Baker was a pleasure. For the record, it brought back many fond memories.

Thank you to US Secret Service special agents and personnel training the men and women at the James J. Rowley Training Center who protect and serve today. I recognized some elements of the training we went through, but boy, it has come a long way! Thank you for letting me take a high-speed ride down Memory Lane, complete with a J-turn at 90 miles per hour. Then, they dusted off an old .357 magnum at the range and let me give it a try. Thank goodness, I still have a good aim. Talk about pressure.

Leaving Utah and growing up in Colorado, I must thank my rifle coach "Teach" Wentworth, who taught me how to competitively shoot while pounding the idea that a "quitter never wins and a winner never quits" into our thick, high school girl heads. It's a good motto when you are writing a book. Thanks to my Centennial High School typing teacher, Mr. Simms. Who knew it would be one of the most import classes I ever took—both for getting me to Washington and writing a book down the road?

To my Colorado cowgirl "posse," Jaelee Pumphrey Jones and Ponce Andres Gebhart: support from friends you've known for more than 50 years and who are still singing your praises is rare. Thank you for all your efforts on my behalf and your constant words of encouragement.

Thank you to the University of Colorado's former Dean of Women, Polly Parish. You pushed me in college to speak up and then made the call that moved me on to Washington. And, thank you to Colorado Congressman Donald Brotzman and his staff for taking a chance on me.

Fifteen years ago, I ran into a young public relations gal, Deb Perry, racing after a film crew to make sure they got just the right shot to tell an important story of the special kids at Driscoll Children's Hospital in Corpus Christi, Texas. Watching her from my post as a "clown" volunteer, I knew she had it covered and that there was more to her story. The fact that she had two small boys, Nick and Sam, and a US Navy F-14 fighter pilot husband who was often times onboard a carrier halfway around the world or serving in Afghanistan for nearly a year didn't scare her. She carried on with gusto, grit, and a twinkle in her eye. Deb inspired me as most military wives tend to do, but she was special.

When I left live television and started a publishing company I knew just enough to get in trouble. I needed a partner, and Deb joined me in our trio of *Snow* books project and became my publicist, my producer, my "mother ship," and my dearest friend. She is the queen of low-to-no budget advertising and marketing. We created, published, and sold more than 150,000 books on a wing and a prayer ... and my American Express card! Her husband, Patrick, retired after twenty years in the navy and they moved to the Pacific Northwest in Camas, Washington, where Deb began booking me all over the country as a keynote speaker. We did this for several years, but my travel was becoming more and more limited because of my husband's Alzheimer's illness.

So we decided to write a book together. Deb is a writer, an editor, an investigator, a charmer, and a teacher, all while still making the basketball games of her two teenage sons and volunteering on every committee at their schools. She tutors algebra—and I know she hates math—and still manages home and hearth while her husband flies the world for Delta Airlines. Thank you to Patrick, Nick, and Sam who have been become like family and have been willing to share her.

Deb is my sounding board and makes what we do possible. For many years it was just the two of us. I would spend hours telling my stories in a written form and send them off to her. I wouldn't suggest I am a professional writer. I write like I talk: in 30-second sound bites, and a lot of them. Deb took my words and turned them into a book. Yes, I found a partner.

Deb is the daughter of US Navy Captain Don Hickman; she calls herself a "navy brat." I believe during his absence during many months at sea, Deb and her mother, Patricia, and two sisters did it scared long before I talked about the concept. She went to multiple schools, was a competitive figure skater, and graduated from Old Dominion University in Norfolk, Virginia. In college, she went out for crew and was selected as a coxswain for both the men's and women's rowing teams. The coxswain sits in the stern, barking out orders and commands, and is responsible for steering the shell and coordinating the power and rhythm of the rowers. Thank you, Deb for being our coxswain!

A simple "thank you" to Cindy Rodriguez just doesn't seem enough for this Girl Friday! She joined us after we signed on with Texas A&M University Press to publish the book. She is a self-starting super woman. I was lucky to find her years ago to help run my husband's psychiatric medical practice, even though she came from an oil and gas background. Then she came onboard to handle the business end of the *Snow* books. But it didn't stop there. Turns out this gal with an affinity for numbers was also as creative as anyone I'd ever worked with. We parted ways when my husband, Cecil, retired, and lucky for Deb and me, she came back to shore up the cavalry charge on another publishing effort and to keep Kathryn out of trouble when she had too much time on her hands.

Thank you to a myriad of people behind the scenes who helped pushed the book to the next level. Pat Jones was the Head of the English Department and English teacher to my son, Clark, at the Hotchkiss School. He credits her with the being the best writing teacher he ever had. Pat came to our aid in the midst of this project. We had gone as far as we could and needed help. She came onboard during rewrite number eight, adding her charm, talent, and editing skills. Now Pat is *my* favorite teacher and dear, dear friend. Talented writer Kelsie Carlstadt came on board with fresh eyes, a youthful take, and willingness to share her writing skills. I knew Cynthia Arbuckle when she was the Features Editor at the daily newspaper, *Corpus Christi Caller-Times,* and always appreciated the stories she wrote and ran. When she agreed to review and polish our work, it gave me hope that we would get published. To this amazing trio of talented ladies—Pat, Kelsey, and Cynthia—thank you from the bottom of my heart for the unending support.

Julie Gordon and Keri Anne Kimbel are my "LA girls" whom I met through my son. Thank you for your tenacity, hard work, and belief that mine was a story that should be told.

Thank you, Kathleen Sullivan, for your ongoing interest and consulting through the years. You inspired us to keep going.

Thank you to Dr. Faye Bruun, a wonderful friend, neighbor from the Beechwood gang, and professor at Texas A&M–Corpus Christi who was willing to read my first draft. She gave me courage when she said to keep going.

Thank you to the remarkable women I call friends, soul mates, and "Clowns." I know you know who you are and are tired of the years I've talked about my "book." You never told me quit ... just sighed and said, "finish the damned thing, and we'll throw you a party." So get out the champagne, girls! The Driscoll Children's Hospital "Clowns Who Care," especially founder Mary Anne Sinclair, Mary Mortimer Campbell, and Chris Adler, are my bulwark, affirming my love of laughter and how stylish you can be wearing greasepaint and a big, red nose. Their support through the writing of this book, and my life in general, has been invaluable. Mary has always been there with sage financial advice, too. So far, it's worked!

Thank you to Susan Corrigan, one of my life-long, dearest friends and fellow clown, whom I lost several years ago. As Lewis Carrol said: "You're entirely bonkers. But I'll tell you a secret ... all the best people are!" She taught me not to take myself so seriously while I was writing and speaking, and it got me through the rough spots.

Bill Wright is a renowned author, photographer, philanthropist, and one of my husband's best friends from Abilene High School. We met up in Marfa, Texas, and I told him about the book. He took a look at it and gave his editor at Texas A&M University Press a call. Thanks, Bill! I hope we did you proud.

I'm told your editor is like your mother. Well, Thom Lemmons, so far so good. Thanks to you and your entire team for taking us on. I sense, like my real father, you will teach us a lot about all of this.

I've always loved folks from Fort Worth, Texas. Remarkably some of my best friends are from "Cowtown." Then I had a chance meeting with Ted Paup after a speech I gave for the James L. West Alzheimer's Foundation—yes, in Fort Worth. As a member of the Advancement Board of Texas A&M University Press, he stepped forward in support of publishing this book—in more ways than one. He and his lovely wife, Nancy, have shown support and interest in my speaking career as well. Thank you both for being my advocates!

Thank you to Zilpha Black who introduced me to Texas and stepped in as Clark's other mother. She taught us both many things. She is my "Yoda," my advisor and oldest friend, and has played an integral part in my life.

Thanks to Linda Valdez for hanging in there with me. We survived a college, life, and category 5 Hurricane Harvey together. What more can you ask?

I have dedicated this book to my sister, Anna Reemsnyder. She is mentioned throughout the book, and I think it is clear I love her dearly and thank her for supporting me in every aspect of my life. Where our mother became somewhat overwhelmed with my "liberation," Anna stepped in. After all, she did find me a husband. Lucky for me, Anna is a writer, a talented editor, and our family historian. Her editing and gentle corrections were invaluable. Anna and her husband, Curt, have been there for me every step of my crazy journey. A doctor who knows something about everything, Curt kept me alive on more than one occasion with astute diagnosis over the phone when I was on assignment somewhere. And he taught me to play tennis!

Seventeen years my senior, my brother, Lee, a brilliant doctor, was off at Columbia University and medical school when I was growing up. He certainly set a high mark, and he and his wife, Pat, were always there for me.

My father, Lealand A. Clark, was my hero. He didn't laugh at me when I said I wanted to grow up and be Annie Oakley. Instead, he smiled and taught me how to do things that most girls weren't allowed to do, like how to shoot and ride an old horse. Thanks to him, I almost believed I was fearless if I just did it scared. I think I got my confidence and ability to tell a good story from him. Ironically, he was the first of many men I would be surrounded by who were all for equal rights for women. My father believed I could do anything, yet encouraged me to remember my mother might have some good points. That's why they had a good marriage.

Thank you to my mother, Ellna Cooper Clark, a remarkable woman. She was of pioneer stock with self-taught traditional elegance, love of good books, and classical music. She loved me with all her heart—and at the same time worried about what would become of me. Her generation walked a tightrope, rearing baby-boomer daughters in a time of so much moral and political change. I think my mother was happy with the way things were. All she wanted for me was stability. Yes, we butted heads over that, but I loved her dearly, and the older I get, the smarter she has become. I laugh when I thank goodness I married Dr. Cecil Childers. In her eyes—and ultimately in mine—he was the best thing that ever happened to me And he brought along a built in "my three sons" family, including Cecil III, Christopher, and Jonathon (who died in a tragic accident in his teens)—all of whom taught me about something I knew little about … stepping up to motherhood.

I was also lucky to have a bird's eye view, watching young Cecil's family blossom when he married Jennifer and added two lovely grandchildren, Ben and Claire. They made good choices and are both Aggies, by the way.

Thank you to Clark Childers and Adam Walton. During most of his adult life, Clark was kind to try to help me with my unhoned writing skills and ambivalence about doing it. There was a lot of handholding over those years. Recently, it was Clark and his husband, Adam Walton, who came to my writing rescue. Both talented and writers with degrees from Brown and Emerson, they were willing to read my "stuff" when I thought I was done. Honestly, Clark had brought me as far as he could. Adam's fresh eyes were particularly helpful. Both gave me honest notes and pushed me to keep rewriting. Their willingness to bear with me, and their love for each other, has made a better person of me. I love them both with all of my heart.

To my husband, Cecil … thank you for your crooked grin, piercing blue eyes, Texas charm, and our fourth son, whom we named Clark Lealand after my father. Ours was a whirlwind, long-distance romance that turned into a life together that lasted over four decades. Both of us were dedicated to something: he to serving and treating the mentally ill, and me to inspiring people to do something they were scared of and creating one project after another until people were exhausted with me. Cecil always said, "Life is too important to take too seriously." He usually followed this statement with a joke—some funny, some not so much. Thank you for being funny, loving and supportive of everything I did—particularly writing this book.

For Cecil's last years, I was his caregiver, filling my days writing while he battled Alzheimer's disease. Working at night in the back of our Airstream trailer during our American tour or in my office at home, he was comfortable as long as I was nearby. Every day he would ask, "Are you finished yet?" I would tell him not yet. "Okay," he would answer and go back to his favorite movie, *Three Amigos.* Today, Cecil would be proud. Yes, honey, I finally finished the book!

SCARED FEARLESS

Prologue

MY HEART beat fast. Looking out, I pressed my head against the tiny window and held my breath. I was home. At first, I was scared to move here. I was alone and didn't know a soul, but I did it anyway. I came to Washington to be a part of something important.

As the jet made its final approach into Washington National Airport (later renamed Ronald Reagan International), the sun seemed to sizzle and sink into the Potomac River. Sunset was the best time to land in the sparkling heart of Washington, DC.

The year was 1972. From the streets to the White House, people were changing the world. Washington was a place of political power and intrigue, and I was at the center of it—working for, and alongside, the most influential people in the world. I had a bad case of "Potomac Fever" and had no interest in getting over it. I was a part of something important and I loved it.

"Are you visiting?" the fellow sitting next to me asked while adjusting his seatbelt, obviously annoyed with the thought of another interloper crowding the roads on his morning commute.

I stowed my flight bag jammed with everything except a *Michelin Guide to Washington on Five Dollars a Day* under the seat. I was not a tourist.

"No, I live here," I said, the words catching in my throat as the Lincoln Memorial, Capitol, and Washington Monument could be seen in the darkness.

The tourists craned their necks to get a look at the landmark bastions of democracy glowing in the darkness. The rest of us, not so much. After all, we lived here.

"Where?"

"On Wisconsin Avenue across from the National Cathedral," I replied.

"Really? Where do you work?" he pried, with a little more interest than before.

As if on cue, the White House appeared deep in the distance.

"There," I said, pointing out the window. "I'm a Secret Service agent."

"Really?" he said again, but more slowly this time. "I didn't know they let girls pull that duty. Actually, I'm not really sure what you do."

"It's a secret," I replied lightheartedly. If I had wanted to, I could have mentioned I'd worked a state dinner at the White House with the Princess of Spain, slipped in a couple of counterfeit undercover buys, and protected John and Caroline Kennedy when they traveled with their mother, former First Lady Jacqueline Kennedy Onassis. Even spent a summer on the island of Scorpios. But I didn't.

With a jolt the tires hit the tarmac and our conversation ended. It was always fun to surprise people, particularly men.

At twenty-four years old, I could hardly believe it myself. I wasn't a tourist or a student at Georgetown University or a secretary on the Hill. I was Special Agent Kathryn Clark, United States Secret Service.

Special Agent Clark—coming home from a protective intelligence assignment. I had been working as an undercover protester on the street at the Democratic and Republican Conventions in Miami. A little tan, a little buff, and with teenage freckles on my nose, no one suspected that I wasn't actually protesting the Vietnam War.

For most of the summer, I and the other agents assigned to the conventions had been living in a quaint vintage hotel on Miami Beach. It had been quite an experience, but I was ready to be home.

The plane landed; passengers stretched, pulled their bags from the overhead compartments, and shuffled to the front of the cabin. My traveling companion turned around and gave me a two-fingered salute.

"Good luck," he said. "Can't wait to tell my wife about you. She's always griping that women don't have much of a chance in this town. We'll see how you do."

"Thanks," I said, shouldering my flight bag and working my way down the aisle. I'd been lucky and was making a little history.

This is my story.

1

Bang!

ACCORDING TO my mother, I was born during an earthquake. She always said she could hear the massive X-ray machines rolling about on the hospital floor above as her IV bag swung like a pendulum on a silver pole. Although I can find no record of an earthquake occurring in Salt Lake City, Utah, in 1947, it made for a good story. If this is ever to be confirmed, it would make for one heck of a foreshadowing for my future.

Earthquake or not, my arrival shook the ground beneath my proud and proper mother's feet. With two grown children—one son already college bound and one teenage daughter—to say I was a surprise is an understatement. My family—hardworking, strong, resilient Mormon stock—were pioneers who had traveled across the plains in wagon trains.

David Cooper, my mother's father, was a blacksmith and worked for the government in the Indian Service near Fort Duchesne, Utah, after the fort's abandonment by the army. As a young woman, my mother taught Native American children to read. My father was a college professor before working as a farm and ranch appraiser. By the time I was born, we lived on a little acreage in the foothills of the Wasatch Range in Pleasant Grove, Utah. Looking back at my life, I laugh when I realize how so much of my early upbringing affected the path I took.

Growing up in the peach tree utopia of Pleasant Grove was idyllic, something out of a storybook. Life was good. I learned to ride a horse, fish, and shinny up the cherry trees to eat the ripe fruit. I had a sweet old plug of a horse named Roxie who pulled ripe apricots off the tree behind our house with her big, slobbery lips. With juice running down her chin, she would spit the seeds out of the side of her mouth as she chewed. Roxie was a patient steed, and she carried both me and the neighbor kids everywhere in the foothills of snowcapped Mount Timpanogos. "Timp" was the highest mountain in the area, and it filled the view from our backyard.

I was loved and content.

My parents came from a conservative background and worked hard to provide a lovely but modest lifestyle. I believed my father, Lealand A. Clark, could do anything, and he believed the same about me. When someone truly believes in you as a kid, it propels you to greatness. He was the kindest man I have ever known.

My father stepped into the backfield of my life, pitching in with the stuff usually reserved for the boys. He taught me I could be a good athlete, and how to drive a nail, cast a fishing rod, ride a horse, and change a tire and put chains on in a snowstorm.

I loved tagging along with him on our two or so acres. Daddy didn't seem to mind, and he continually gave me chances to learn things that most girls didn't. I helped him irrigate the pastures, feed the sheep, and mend the fences.

When he passed away I found one of his well-worn business cards with a message typed on the back. I don't know whether it was original to him or borrowed, but it fits him and I have used it over the years.

> As you grow older
> Have the strength to be tender
> The wisdom to laugh
> The compassion to be tolerant
> And the integrity to speak the truth

I was also reared by three strong yet traditional women—my grandma; my mother, Ellna; and my sister, Anna. The trio tried with all their might to make a "proper" girl out of me, encouraging me to learn to sew, play the piano, and accessorize dolls. It is reported I was well behaved, but the rest didn't come naturally.

My grandma was truly a pioneer woman with a huge heart. She was a talented seamstress. I heard she had created elegant hats for the president of the Mormon Church and Brigham Young's wives as a young woman growing up in Salt Lake City. Ellna, my mother, was a brilliant woman—an accomplished violinist and a natural and exceptional teacher. My sister and I have often said she was born at the wrong time. Had the women's movement surfaced when she was a young woman with opportunities on the horizon, I believe her life could have been very different. She surely had the gumption, but I fear she would have struggled with the evolving standards attached to being a woman in the 1970s.

My sister, Anna, was the proper girl my mother and grandmother hoped I'd grow into; she was an accomplished pianist and could bake a perfect angel food cake. At four years old, I loved to sit on the counter and watch her froth the whites using Mother's eggbeater, then pour a teaspoon of mysterious dark liquid from a tiny bottle into the bowl. The smell of the vanilla made my mouth water. I so wanted to taste it. Banging my high-topped leather-laced shoes against the cupboards below I whined and begged for a spoonful. "You won't like it, Kathy," Anna would say patiently above the roar of the beaters.

"Yes I will," I cried. Fourteen years my senior, my sister helped raise me and continues to be my best friend. Kindly observing my bad behavior, she insisted, "No you won't," adding a bit of sternness to her voice.

But I wouldn't give up. Finally, she pulled a well-worn tablespoon from the drawer and filled it to the top.

"Okay," she said. "Here you go."

I couldn't wait. I grabbed the handle and shoved the spoon in my mouth. With a gasp, I screwed up my face and spit it out, all over the two of us. She smiled and began the cleanup process. We both laughed.

That day, Anna taught me that if something smells good, it won't necessarily taste good. I've never forgotten that life lesson. And yes, it was early training for my job as a special agent. Things are not always as they appear. In the Secret Service, I further learned that if something doesn't look right, it probably isn't. Along with our extensive training, we were taught to trust our instincts when we were protecting and serving the president of the United States. I can assure you, I never asked for a taste of straight vanilla again.

I always depended on a sense of humor to get over the rough spots with anyone. My mother and father honed those skills early in their little girl growing up. When I failed to be picked for the cheerleading squad, mother brought her kind salve of comfort, saying "laugh and the world laughs with you, cry and you cry alone," and giving me a clean hankie to blow my nose on and a tight squeeze to say how proud she was of me anyway.

My father always had a twinkle in his eye and could befriend anyone. I traveled with him when I was a kid on some of his visits to ranches he was appraising. A nice break in the afternoon was to stop at a random café along the way for a cup of coffee and a nickel Coke for me. I noticed how he always greeted the waitress as an old friend whether he knew her or not. Wiping the counter with a wet hand towel, she looked exhausted. It was probably the end of a long one and she was ready to call it a day. Slapping down the maroon plastic-covered menus that stuck to the counters, she said, "What'll ya have?" while pulling a stub of a pencil from behind her ear where a white cap of sorts hid wisps of gray hair. Daddy would usually start the conversation with "Boy I'll bet you're tired. How do your feet feel?" Before I knew it, a tiny smile would be creeping into the lines around her lips and a fresh pot of coffee and the last two pieces of cherry pie would make their way in front of our stools. It worked every time. My father taught me that being genuinely nice and genuinely interested in people worked. If I have one trait I'm proud of, it would be that one.

I tell this story because my experience of being one of the first women in a world of men took all the skills I could muster.

I had a perfect childhood. My mother did everything within her power to give me the traditional background she assumed I would need growing up: good taste, music lessons, high values, and lots of love. But as I grew up, the unconditional part was harder for her. Preparing me to "rock the boat" was not something she had planned on. But as I look back at our lives together, I realize she was proud of what I did. When she was older, perhaps her beautiful white hair was a sign of her struggle with the changes going on in humankind—particularly womankind—and her struggle to adapt to them.

At forty-five, between teaching school and taking classes to earn her degree at Brigham Young University, my mother canned deer meat from the fall hunt in glass mason jars in her spare time. Can't say I liked it! It was red and the fat floated like white spiders in the broth. I did, however, like the homemade yeast-based root beer my sister and I brewed in recycled glass bottles. The process wasn't perfect, and every so often, the fermenting brew we kept in a dark closet would explode.

My grandma lived with us and canned peaches. The smell of baking bread in the oven greeted me every day when I came home from school. She always gave me the heel of the loaf, slathered in butter and homemade strawberry jam.

When I was six years old, I didn't like playing with dolls; I preferred to dress kittens in clothes and push them about in a buggy. I did have a Betsy Wetsy "drink-and-wet" doll. It was one of the most popular dolls of its kind in 1953, the baby doll of choice for little girls. But my interest in Betsy was short-lived when I realized playing with her meant changing and washing her tiny cotton diapers. Anna surprised me once by scooping a teaspoon of pumpkin pie filling into one of them, and I quickly resigned my nanny job. Oh, well—that came later, and the travel and benefits were much better.

After Betsy, I moved on to my new favorite thing—a full-blown replica of Smokey Bear complete with a hat, shovel, silver belt buckle, and gold badge. His message was emblazoned across the giant cellophane-wrapped box he came in: "Remember, only YOU can prevent forest fires." I can remember thinking his life was far more interesting than lying around with pumpkin pie in your diapers.

When adults asked me what I wanted to be when I grew up, I was stumped. Then my sister read the story of Smokey Bear to me. He survived a terrible forest fire as a cub and became the "spokesbear" for the US Forest Service. He lived in the National Zoo in Washington, DC, and was the most famous bear alive. I thought that sounded exciting. Maybe I could be a forest ranger when I grew up, I thought, but there was no mention of a "girl" Smokey Bear.

I wasn't sure where Washington, DC, was, but I knew it was a long way from Utah. I believed my mother when she said I couldn't become a forest ranger or move to Washington, because "girls don't do that." It was ingrained in me early on that girls weren't allowed to do the things I found fun and interesting.

Then I learned about Annie Oakley. She was my answer, my goal, my muse. I wanted to be her when I grew up. She was a real cowgirl who had grown up much like me. She didn't like to play with dolls. She much preferred to hunt with her father and spend time outdoors. She was a sure shot with a rifle, and one of the best in the world by the time she was a teenager. I thought that was something!

Annie offered to join the US Army during World War I but was told, "Thank you, girls don't do that." Wanting to use her shooting skills to serve her country, she wrote a letter to President McKinley in 1898 offering to fight for the United States in the Spanish-American War. She never got a response. Apparently, shooting was reserved for men and boys.

Annie was one of a kind. She was perhaps the most famous woman in the West, and she was tough yet maintained her femininity. She didn't dress or behave like a man to fit in. She wore pretty pearl earrings with her cowboy hat and fringed jacket. She traveled the world riding in the Buffalo Bill Wild West Show and met some of the most important people in the world—kings, queens, and, in 1884, the Sioux chief Sitting Bull.

Acknowledging both her height and her shooting skill, Sitting Bull nicknamed her "Little Sure Shot." She was only five feet tall and wouldn't have been tall enough to be a Secret Service agent. Luckily for me, I was five feet eight inches and got to meet my share of royals and presidents and see the world, but I never met an Indian chief.

I read everything I could about her. I dreamed of riding Roxie at full gallop while grasping the pole of an American flag flapping in the breeze. We were leading the grand entry into the Pleasant Grove Strawberry Days Rodeo. One problem, though—Roxie wouldn't gallop, and unfortunately, little girls weren't supposed to do that either. Instead, I was chosen to ride on a float in the parade while dressed as a demure Betsy Ross with an American flag draped across my lap. No flag flapping.

By the time I was seven years old, I thought I was well on my way to life beyond parade floats. I had worked with Roxie in the back pasture, wildly kicking her bulging sides with my well-worn cowboy boots. We managed an occasional trot, and my border collie, Tippy, walked behind creating what I imagined was my own Wild West Show grand entry. I became a good rider in the process. Years later when I protected Caroline Kennedy on a proper fox hunt in York, England, I think I could have stayed on the horse. Luckily, the advance agent had failed to arrange for one for me and I didn't have to prove it.

At this point in my childhood, I desperately wanted to learn to shoot my father's .22 rifle. Annie had started shooting when she was eight. Every year, Daddy and my brother, who was seventeen years my senior, went bird hunting. The girls were never invited. I was too little and my sister had no interest.

Finally, during the summer of 1954, I got to shoot that gun. Daddy was working on a fence he had made from old World War II tent posts and was painting them white. He was busy, but I was insistent. "Would you teach me to shoot the rifle?" I begged.

Chuckling, Daddy said, "Now?"

I nodded yes.

"Okay," he obliged me; I think he respected my tenacity and was amused by my resolve. "I suppose the paint needs to dry a bit."

We walked to the house, and he found the old gun in the back of a musty closet filled with a mishmash of boots, jackets, and hunting gear that smelled of cleaning oil and gunpowder. Reaching deep into a shelf near the top, he grabbed a tattered green and white box of brass .22 shells with shiny copper tips. He stuck a handful in his shirt pocket. Leaving the house, he grabbed a can from the garbage and stripped off the label as we walked down the dirt road.

"Are you sure you want to do this?" Daddy asked.

"Yes," I said, bobbing my head. I knew this experience would put me one step closer to my Annie Oakley dream.

"Okay," he said, placing the shiny can on a fence post twenty feet or so from where I stood.

Handing me the gun, he told me to snug the butt into my shoulder, look down the sight, and center the little bead at the end of the barrel just below the bottom of the can.

"Breathe in, breathe out, then squeeze the trigger," Daddy said calmly.

Until the gun was actually in my little hands, I'd been excited. But it was much heavier than I expected. It was not a toy and came with lots of responsibility attached. If I didn't shoot the gun properly, I would get hurt, or worse—I would hurt someone else. That reverence for the weapon and the burden of wielding it affected me both then and in the years to come.

My cowgirl bravado faded, and my heart beat fast. I did the best I could to wrap my little fingers around the girth of the .22. Its barrel smelled of gunpowder. There was also another stench—one of danger, cold and real.

I did as Daddy said and stretched the index finger of my right hand to pull back the trigger. It was more difficult than I anticipated, so I released it.

"I'm scared," I mumbled.

"That's okay," he said, lifting the gun out of my wobbly grip. "You don't have to shoot it today. Maybe you're not ready. Maybe you aren't old enough. Maybe you really don't want to. It's your choice."

"No," I said. "I'm just scared."

Tears rolled down my cheeks.

"Well then," my father said, "just do it scared."

He returned the gun to my hands. I snugged it into my shoulder, took a deep breath, and decided to be brave. I aimed and squeezed the trigger, nice and slow.

Bang!

The can jumped five feet in the air, and I was hooked. It was difficult, but I was hooked on doing something I didn't think I could do. Doing what scared me was exhilarating. I was excited and motivated by overcoming that little voice in my head that told me, "You're just a girl. You're too small. You can't do that."

Yes I can. Yes I did. Yes I would. As a girl, in spite of being a girl, and because I was a girl, I would do it all.

Even as a United States Secret Service agent shooting on the range in the basement of the Treasury Building, pulling the trigger of my service revolver was difficult. The .357 Magnum revolver was not designed to fit a woman's hand. Sometimes I would release the trigger, take a deep breath, and start again. Although I was good at it, I often thought I wouldn't qualify and hit the target in the "kill zone." It was more than just a bang. The air would fill with the violent sound of the explosion inside the gun I held as it launched the bullet toward the paper target. More often than not, I hit the target and was excited that I could, but I never got over being scared.

Remarkably, my decision to try something new despite my fear led me down a path to a career that didn't even exist at the time. It provided a place in the history books when I became one of the first five young women who took the oath as Secret Service special agents, becoming the first of our sex to join the 100-plus-year-old agency.

2

A Girl with Gumption

MY FATHER was transferred from Utah to Pueblo, Colorado, when I was in the fourth grade. The move required leaving behind my horse, my dog, and my dreams of being Annie Oakley. But I noticed that Daddy did slip the old .22 under a blanket in the trunk of the car. With tears, I looked back at my perfect life, feeling that I was leaving everything that mattered to me.

As it turns out, I brought more with me from Pleasant Grove than I realized. Although it was small, my "growing up" suitcase was filled with the bravado, curiosity, and knowledge my father had instilled in me. Just the trappings I needed for an exciting life. That skill set, however, does little for success in a fifth-grade popularity contest.

I knew my father was an advocate for my "I can do anything" attitude. On the other hand, my mother and most other mothers in the 1960s didn't believe being on equal footing with men was as important as marrying one. My mother was concerned about what other people would think. She loved me and wanted to make a well-educated, well-behaved lady of me.

The popular girls were pretty and shorter than the boys, had small feet, and were in training to be cheerleaders. I, in turn, was tall and athletic, with freckles on my nose, and had larger feet than most girls. I used to dutifully ink out the printed numbers inside my shoes. When boys asked me to go bowling, there was another problem. Rental shoes announced one's size in giant red letters on the backs of the shoes. Then when I would tell my mother I had outscored the boys, she would suggest it might be more to my advantage to go to the movies instead. Turns out my shoe size was unimportant and may have been a good thing. I read once that Jacqueline Kennedy Onassis's shoe size wasn't particularly small and no one seemed to care.

When I was a teenager, my best friend, Jaelee Pumphrey, invited me to go skiing with her family. She had three brothers, and they adopted me as the "take-along sister." Skiing was not a cheap sport, but Daddy was creative. The army surplus store sold old military skis made of oak with long thong bindings. He bought them secondhand and we painted them red. I wrapped the six-foot-long straps of leather as tight as I could around my boots.

Our weekend pastime led into competition when Pueblo's Centennial High School ski team allowed girls to join in on the fun. I won only a few downhill races, but I relished the competition and loved going fast. After a run, my legs felt like rubber, and my face turned red and became chapped from the cold or because I forgot to breathe. When it was icy on the mountain, it took all my strength to make wide turns, digging the metal edges of the skis into the ice, carving a line across a steep hill. It was exhilarating.

Trying out for the National Ski Patrol was my first "token girl" experience. To qualify, we had to be top skiers and able to negotiate any run on the mountain. First, we convinced the patrol that we had the endurance to climb the mountain; then we had to prove we had the strength to bring an injured three-hundred-pound male skier off the mountain in a sled we controlled with our skis in a wedge like a snowplow. We spent months in first aid and rescue classes. We learned how to treat injuries and save lives.

Our sophomore year in high school, Jaelee and I passed the course and were the first girls asked to join the National Ski Patrol on Monarch Pass near Gunnison, Colorado. It was the first time being an athletic girl would come in handy—and it wouldn't be the last. As a teenager, I helped ensure skier safety; we learned how to work avalanches and search for missing skiers. At the end of the day after the lift had closed, our job was to make the last run to be sure that everyone had made it off the mountain. No matter the weather, we went up the mountain when others were coming down.

Since we were under eighteen, we were designated Junior Patrol, but we had the same responsibilities and worked just as hard as the adults, all of whom were men. We were proud but at the time, the best part for us was we got to ski free.

Dressed in jeans and red jackets with a white cross on the back, carrying a bag of first aid supplies around our waists, we looked like the seasoned skiers that we were. Around Christmas break, the Texas Young Life girls arrived by the busload, dressed in white Bogner ski pants and matching jackets. Each year, at least one blonde "ski bunny" would break her leg on her first run. I was generally summoned on those calls since I carried a seam ripper in my bag so that we wouldn't have to cut the pants off to treat her leg. In many cases, the poor girl was much more concerned about her outfit than the break. The guys just didn't understand. I did. I would have killed for a pair of those pants.

In the years to come, I was beyond grateful for my many winters in Colorado. When I skied with Caroline Kennedy in the Austrian Alps, instead of a seam ripper in my pack, I carried my service revolver. I was prepared to use it should I need to protect her. I'll admit it worried me that if I took a fall the gun might go off, but I never fell. She was a great skier, and I had to keep up and I did.

Unfortunately, there were few athletic opportunities for high school girls in the early 1960s. At the time, there was no Title IX legislation requiring federally funded schools to provide equal opportunities for women to get into the game. Quite simply, equal opportunities were not available in many arenas—sports or otherwise.

My brother-in-law, Curt, taught me how to play tennis, but there wasn't a girls' team at my high school, so they "let me" play with the boys and warm them up for their matches. Fortunately, I was invited to join and play on a state-wide, select-only squad, and I competed in matches around the state. It was one of the few opportunities for women to compete in our area, and I loved it.

Just like my skiing ability, my tennis skills came in handy during Caroline's Austrian summer camp. Onlookers would never have assumed that the woman on the courts in a tennis dress was Caroline's undercover bodyguard. It would have been more difficult for a male agent to surreptitiously warm Caroline up for her lesson with Chuck McKinley, the world's number one men's amateur tennis champion of the 1960s. He was a nice guy and didn't make me look bad when I hit with him. Of course, he wanted to know where I kept my gun. I told him it was a secret, but then he eyed my flight bag near the corner of the back line. It was filled with yellow tennis balls and was unusually heavy.

One afternoon while playing dodge ball in high school gym class, Coach "Teach" Wentworth approached me. Everyone was afraid of this older, wiser woman. She had a nice smile when she used it but was better known for her no-nonsense approach to coaching. I'll admit, she scared me. "Kathy," she barked. "Have you ever considered trying out for our Girl's Rifle Club?"

In passing, I'd mentioned that I knew how to shoot. "Not really," I replied. "I'm more into skiing, but I do like shooting. I always have."

"Come to the range after school, and let's see how you do," she replied.

The range was a long, narrow, musty length of creaky hardwood in the basement. There was barely room for two girls, clad in shooting jackets emblazoned with a Centennial High School Bulldog Girl's Rifle Club patch over the left pocket, to take aim and shoot. Coach Wentworth pulled a jacket off a peg on the wall, and I put it on. She handed me an antique-looking bolt action .22 rifle and a handful of brass-cased shells. I loaded the gun, took a deep breath, and exhaled just like Daddy taught me. I watched carefully as the sight at the end of the barrel danced around the bottom of the target.

Squeeze, squeeze, squeeze—bang! It was a good shot. Actually, it was a great shot.

Once again, I was hooked. At that moment, I decided to join the team.

Coach Wentworth was not the tough old bird she liked to portray. She was actually very nice. Her motto, "A winner never quits and a quitter never wins," was emblazoned on a canvas banner that hung on the wall at the end of the range. On more than one occasion she prodded me, "You could be really good at this if you work hard enough."

"You think so?" I asked, looking for reassurance.

"Shooting competitions are tough. They're won or lost by the slightest margin. You must practice and be committed to be good at it. And you've got to have gumption," she said with a twinkle in her eye.

"What's gumption?"

"Well," she said, "it means being savvy and a little gutsy. Sometimes you should be resourceful, clever, and have the backbone to think outside of the box. Some people call it moxie or horse sense. It means you have to take the initiative to do things a lot of girls are afraid to try."

"And I have it? Gumption?"

"Yes," she continued, and her words resonated with me. "You absolutely have it. Use it! Particularly when you shoot against the boys. They don't think you have the right to compete. After all, you are *just a girl*." She laughed, and I couldn't help but smile.

Later that month we advanced to the Colorado State Rifle Championship where boys and girls were competing against one another. I noticed that a line of boys seemed to be more stable shooting in a standing position. They were wearing heavy shoes with, of course, bigger feet filling them, and their scores were higher than mine.

"Hey, Teach," I called out. "Any rules about what kind of shoes you wear when you're competing?"

"Not that I know of," she grumbled.

"I have an idea," I replied, and I ran to the bus where I happened to have stowed my ski boots for skiing later that day. Lacing them on before the next round, I clomped out to take my position. Now I had a more stable platform just like the boys. I won the Colorado State Rifle Championship that year in the girls' division and beat most of the boys' scores, too!

As I climbed on the bus wearing my ski boots with a trophy under my arm, Coach Wentworth patted me on the back and gave me a wink and a smile.

"Congratulations, Kathy," she said. "You've got gumption and you always will."

That day, inspired by the first of many times, I had to get creative to level the playing field in a man's world. I embraced both my gumption and my shoe size.

3

Duck and Cover

I WAS LUCKY to have grown up in the 1950s—a time when people were hopeful and ready to put the Great Depression and World War II behind them. I loved the *Saturday Evening Post* and the covers illustrated by Norman Rockwell. In 1956, Rockwell's painting of President Dwight Eisenhower appeared on the cover; the dog-eared magazine earned a special spot on the coffee table in our living room for months. My parents adored "Ike," our kind, fatherlike president. Nothing bad was going to happen on his watch—President Eisenhower said so.

Times were good—families had money to build a home in the growing suburbs and stock it with a ninety-nine-dollar black-and-white television, a twelve-inch magic box that would influence our lives not unlike the internet does today. Everything revolved around the television. We didn't know how it worked and we didn't care. With the turn of a knob, a TV set could bring *The Mickey Mouse Club*, a children's show, and *American Bandstand*, the most popular dance party in the United States, into our living rooms. Reportedly, half the US population watched Disneyland's grand opening on July 17, 1955, broadcast live from Anaheim, California, on their new TV sets.

Then along came Elvis Presley. He joined the party with a new kind of music called rock and roll and sent shock waves around the country with his soulful singing, wild hip gyrations, and raw energy, attracting record-breaking audiences when he appeared on television shows such as *The Ed Sullivan Show*. The term "rock and roll" was first used in 1951 by Alan Freed, a Cleveland disc jockey, who took it from the song "My Baby Rocks Me with One Steady Roll." Most parents were horrified when they figured out what the kids knew all along—rock and roll meant sex. At the time, I was a little girl and too young to care, so I went outside and saddled up my horse.

Although sex and the Sexual Revolution were creeping into the picture, my mother and father never spoke of it. Like the Cold War, I guess they thought it would just go away. I was thirteen years old when a tiny blue pill was made available in 1960. It was initially marketed as a cure for severe menstrual cramps, and millions of girls immediately started having symptoms. When it was shown to prevent pregnancy—Katie, bar the door! But not for this Katie. Even though my brother, an MD at the time, gave me a prescription when I started high school, I didn't trust the pill. I wasn't convinced it would really work, and that scared me.

During high school, I didn't have a steady boyfriend and couldn't afford to get pregnant. Yet it became clear you probably wouldn't get a husband or a steady date without having sex. Even then, there was no guarantee of a ring on your finger if you did get pregnant. Abortions were illegal, and girls died from botched procedures. Having a child out of wedlock was typically the kiss of death. A girl was sent to a home for unwed mothers and then had to give up the infant for adoption. If she chose to keep the baby, she simply disappeared. In the United States, well into the 1960s, a child's birth certificate might be stamped "bastard" if there was no father listed and it was born out of wedlock. Raising a child as a single parent in those days was not a socially acceptable option and rarely happened.

The thought of telling my parents I was pregnant was unthinkable. I am not making light of it when I say I would have considered suicide my only option had I gotten pregnant. I realize now why our mothers were so anxious for their daughters to marry. We were all in a dilemma.

As magical as TV was, it also opened the door to daily newscasts, and the news wasn't all good. With a turn of a clunky knob, my parents could choose between two fifteen-minute newscasts—the CBS evening news with Douglas Edwards or NBC's *Camel News Caravan* with John Cameron Swayze. Swayze was required by the tobacco company sponsor to have a burning cigarette always visible when he was on camera. There was no mention that cigarettes could kill you in those days, but a lot of talk that the Cold War might.

In 1950, North Korea invaded South Korea, and some dads in the neighborhood were called to serve in the army. My father was too old and didn't have to serve. I was glad. The Korean War increased efforts in the United States to develop a bomb even more deadly that the atomic bomb used in World War II. The Russians tested their own atomic bomb, and the nuclear race began as Russia and the United States competed to build more and better weapons of mass destruction. I didn't realize it then, but this was the beginning of a deadly race.

As I entered the fifth grade, parents and teachers were concerned about a nuclear war with Russia. Our PTA had a bake sale and raised enough money to outfit us with dog tags—in case they needed to identify our bodies after a bomb was dropped on our hometown. Students went through weekly civil defense drills.

"Crouch under the desk, cover your head to protect yourself from the blast, then run to the curb where your mother will pick you up and drive you to the mountains," the principal would instruct us.

I don't remember being afraid. The drills were something we did, along with watching the World Series if we finished our math. Eventually, they put an end to the civil defense drills in junior high. I guess someone figured out that the duck-and-cover maneuver wouldn't work against an atomic bomb anyway.

In 1960, John F. Kennedy was elected president at the young age of forty-three. He was the first president I remember well. He was loved by most of the country. His predecessor, Dwight D. Eisenhower, was my parents' favorite. My mother loved Mamie, President Eisenhower's wife. "She is lovely, lady-like, and always stood several paces behind the president like a woman should," my mother declared.

I instinctively liked Jacqueline Kennedy. She was thirty-one when President Kennedy took office. Instead of standing behind him, she moved to the forefront. Mother thought it was terrible that she "upstaged" the president in France and other places, deeming her "uppity." I thought she was remarkable. Years later, when I met her and had the opportunity to know her, my early observations were affirmed. My mother wasn't ready for women to stand alongside men, different but equal, but I wanted to be. Why shouldn't the first lady stand alongside her husband? She was a change maker, an icon, and often revered as much as the president himself.

During that time, Khrushchev and the Russians were our enemies. We were told we were in the midst of the Cold War, fighting the Iron Curtain. I never quite grasped what all that meant until my sophomore year in high school. On October 22, 1962, President Kennedy announced to the nation on our grainy TV that the Russians were installing missiles in Cuba, and they were pointed at us. He began the seventeen-minute speech with "My fellow citizens . . ." When a president begins a speech this way, he generally does not have good news. Kennedy warned us that "the path we have chosen is full of hazards, as all paths are." Although I agree with this sentiment now, as a high school girl, all I heard was that World War III was about to start, and we were going to die.

The morning after President Kennedy's announcement, my girlfriends and I were huddled in front of our lockers talking in hushed tones. Ostensibly, we were talking about the Cuban Missile Crisis, but in reality we were talking about sex. Looking back, I see it was a cover—something to do while we waited for the end of the world, knowing we would die before we had sex. A few of the wild girls had steady boyfriends and knew more about sex than the rest of us. Most of us were saving ourselves for the boy we would marry. All we had done was go around one or two of the proverbial bases—first, second, and for a very few, third.

A little over a year after the Cuban Missile Crisis—around noon on November 22, 1963—the scratching of No. 2 pencils on a purple mimeographed pop quiz in history class was interrupted by a tapping on the microphone of our PA system. The principal cleared his throat. Then he cleared it a second time. Taking a deep breath, he said simply, "Attention all students . . . the president has been shot in Dallas, Texas."

We put down our pencils. Centennial High School went into emotional lockdown, a word we didn't even know back then. We were scared about what would happen next—scared that the world we knew would never be the same. I bet everyone alive that day remembers where he or she was, in heart- and gut-wrenching detail.

Schools closed, businesses closed—even the state championship football game was canceled. Yet everyone did the best he or she could to carry on. It was the first time I saw boys cry. An event of this magnitude had not happened to us, and we didn't know what to do.

Jaelee and I spent the next five days sitting on the Pumphreys' turquoise shag carpet watching their television. We saw Walter Cronkite wipe a tear from his eye when he announced that President Kennedy was dead.

Many years later I interviewed Mr. Cronkite in his New York City office for my morning television show. He told me that news anchors don't shed tears on the air, but that day he did. It was a rare and touching conversation I doubt would have happened had he not known I had been a special agent who protected the Kennedy children.

Jaelee and I watched Mrs. Kennedy, in the now unforgettable blood-stained suit she had been wearing when the president was shot, stand next to Vice President Lyndon B. Johnson on Air Force One as he took the oath of office to become president. Secret Service agent Clint Hill stood behind them and watched.

At the time, I had no idea what the Secret Service was or what special agents did. All I knew was that this man, Special Agent Clinton J. Hill, would forever be remembered for his extraordinary act of bravery on the back of the presidential limousine in Dallas that day. When gunfire erupted, Agent Hill jumped from the follow-up car and leaped onto the trunk of the accelerating presidential limousine. He crawled to Mrs. Kennedy and guided the first lady back into her seat. Once back in the car, Hill placed his body over the president and Mrs. Kennedy. Hill later told the Warren Commission that he thought Mrs. Kennedy was in shock and was reaching for a piece of the president's skull. What I didn't know was that Special Agent Hill would eventually become the assistant director of the Secret Service and would hire me.

During the funeral procession, the entire country watched Mrs. Kennedy bravely walk down Pennsylvania Avenue, her face swollen beneath a dark veil. The president's brothers, Robert and Edward, walked near her. A sleek riderless horse, "Black Jack," carrying highly polished boots reversed in the stirrups, pranced in the middle of the street, the unmistakable symbol of a fallen leader.

Mrs. Kennedy walked slowly behind an antique gun carriage caisson, which had carried President Lincoln after he had been assassinated and now carried the body of her husband, to Arlington National Cemetery. Mrs. Kennedy's daughter, Caroline, and her younger son, John, walked beside her, followed by world leaders from France, Germany, Belgium, Ireland, and Ethiopia. Former presidents Truman and Eisenhower were also present.

At one point, young John stood in front of St. Matthew's Cathedral and snapped a salute with his little gloved hand as his father's body passed by on that morning of November 25, 1963, the boy's third birthday. In my mind, it was the most poignant, heartbreaking moment from an unprecedented four-day stretch of American history. The enormity of the event—the people, the times, our future, and the future of the free world—washed over us like the tears rolling down our collective cheeks.

I was scared. The country was scared. We were all in disbelief. The world we knew seemed to be crumbling to the beat of the drums in the funeral procession. So continued the 1960s—turbulent, trying, and, yes, revolutionary times.

A few weeks later, the Colorado State Football Championship was rescheduled, and we carried on. I don't remember whether we won or not. In the greater scheme of things, it wasn't important. Life wasn't the same. The Vietnam War had ramped up. Boys I dated were sent off to fight. Several never came back. Dr. Martin Luther King Jr.'s dream for an equal black and white America and the women's movement moved to the forefront of our cultural revolution.

A Rockwell portrait of President Kennedy appeared in 1963 on the cover of the *Saturday Evening Post*, a week after the president's assassination. Some say that's when the age of our nation's collective innocence ended.

The assassination of President Kennedy was life changing. Although I could not fathom it at the time, it would have a profound impact on my personal life. In the aftermath of his death, the Secret Service made the hiring of female agents one of many changes to the protection of the president and his family. I would be the one who protected his children.

On May 29, 2017, President Kennedy would have turned one hundred years old. I hit seven decades in October 2017. I lived through much of the legacy he left from his brief 1,038 days in office and admire greatly what he was able to accomplish and set into motion.

Upon the one-hundredth anniversary of his birth, the John F. Kennedy Presidential Library and Museum published this statement:

> In his brief time in office, President Kennedy mobilized a genera-
> tion to serve their country. He championed equality, averted nucle-
> ar disaster, celebrated the arts, and challenged us to work together

to achieve the impossible. Together with Jacqueline Kennedy, he inspired millions of people around the world with his vision of a New Frontier. President Kennedy inspired a generation to accept responsibility for its government, and its world, by taking political and social action. As President, he fought to ensure equal rights and opportunities for all Americans. He encouraged Americans to lift up those less fortunate than themselves, both at home and abroad. He challenged the nation to reach for the impossible and land a man on the moon before the end of the decade. He set new directions for international diplomacy, seeking better relations with Latin America and newly independent nations. He reduced the threat of nuclear war by opening the lines of communication with Moscow and offering to help make the world safe for diversity.

I am proud to have called John F. Kennedy my president and to have served to protect his children.

4

The Times They Are A-Changin'

IN THE 1960S, if the parents could afford it, many families sent their daughters to college. Most often, it was to get a BS in education in order to teach school along with the suggested degree of choice, an "MRS degree." A teaching career would allow me to put my future husband through medical school, law school, or similar training. Graduate schools didn't offer many spots for women and were rarely in the discussion of a girl's higher education. "You can either be a teacher, a nurse, or an old maid," a freshman friend of mine quipped once as she headed out to a party.

My parents had worked hard and saved to send me to college. The summer of 1965, I enrolled at the University of Colorado (CU) in Boulder. I had no idea what I wanted to do with my life. I just hoped "interesting" would be found somewhere in the description. To appease my parents, I majored in elementary education. I came from great teacher stock and knew I would at least be good at it and could always use it later.

CU was a large university and when my father moved me into the dorm, I didn't know a soul. I decided to go through rush and joined Gamma Phi Beta, a sorority, even though I knew little about it. Turns out it was the best thing I could have done. Gamma Phi was a complete package of friends, fun, and yes—demanding study halls. Living at the sorority house created a built-in family for me at a huge university far from home. Many of us remain great friends today. And the fraternities provided cute boys to date, too!

The historic events that defined my final two years at CU would impact my life in ways I never could have dreamed. The days leading into the 1970s were tumultuous, filled with conflicting emotion. In some ways, the decade was a continuation of the 1960s. Women, African Americans, Native Americans, gays and lesbians, and other sidelined people continued their fight for equality, and many Americans joined the protest against the ongoing war in Vietnam. There were lots of voices out there and I was one of them.

Something I hadn't counted on was the leadership opportunities at the university when I was elected president of the Panhellenic Council, an organization that oversees the actions of all the sororities on campus. Another Gamma Phi, Linda Valdez, had held the job before me and taught me the ropes.

If I had communication skills when I left school, I learned them leading this sharp group of sorority women from across campus at a time when the Greek system was struggling. We were a tight-knit and diverse group. Linda "Ponce" Andres Gebhart, a Phi Beta Phi, and I became the best of friends and shared our dreams of "doing something important" when we graduated. And we did. We both moved to Washington, taking the leadership skills we'd learned at the university to Capitol Hill. I worked for a congressman. Ponce joined the staff of a senator. We were roommates and both drove used VW Beetles—the car of choice in 1969. We are still best friends today.

Without even really knowing it, I was forging the interesting life I had hoped for. Of all the girls in my pledge class, I may not have been the one pegged to forge a new path for women. I hadn't worn the T-shirt declaring I was a "women's libber." I wasn't a hippie, either. I was what they called a "nonmilitant conservative," taking a stand in my own way. I was looking for a way to make an impact from the inside out. That was a bigger challenge than you would think. After all the dust settled, I gave a cheer for the brave, boisterous girls who brought the idea of equality to the forefront. Without them, I wouldn't have had the chance to join the ranks of change.

The antigovernment protests distressed me; they were unpatriotic. I believed we were doing what needed to be done in Vietnam. If women had been allowed in the military at the time, I would have joined. I would have loved to attend the Air Force Academy in Colorado Springs up the road from my home. Instead I often served as the university-appointed on-campus spokesperson for the nonmilitant conservatives when the press wanted to interview a student. There were always two sides to the dialogue, and I prayed our government knew what it was doing.

Everywhere I looked, regular people and elected officials were demanding and defining a new normal, and we struggled to know what to do with it. The hippies grew out their hair, pulled on discarded military garb, and took to the streets. Women's liberation girls were said to burn their bras in protest, but I never saw one do it. The Students for a Democratic Society almost closed the school over a national convention they wanted to hold on campus.

I well remember 1968, my junior year at CU. Our world was rattled as Bob Dylan sang "The Times They Are A-Changin'." The last verse said it all:

> The line is drawn
> The curse it is cast
> The slow one now
> Will later be fast
> As the present now
> Will later be past
> The order is rapidly fading
> And the first one now will later be last
> For the times they are a-changin'

On April 4, 1968, a lone assassin shot Reverend Martin Luther King Jr. as he was standing on the balcony of the Lorraine Motel in Memphis. Race riots followed and we watched poor areas in Washington and Los Angeles burn on the broadcasts of the evening news. Reports on Vietnam followed, showing ragged photographs of the piles of dead Vietnamese fighters complete with daily body counts.

Two months later, on June 5, 1968, several of us sat on the floor at our housemother's apartment watching her TV. US senator and presidential candidate Robert "Bobby" F. Kennedy thanked a room packed with cheering, sweating supporters wearing white spinner hats and ribbons emblazoned with "KENNEDY" while they screamed, "Hip hip hooray, RFK!" They were young like us.

"I wish we could be there," my friend Elizabeth commented.

"So many people. You'd think they were at a Beatles concert."

We were mesmerized. Robert Kennedy seemed to be everything his brother was, and perhaps more. "This is going to change things," I remember thinking. Little did I know how much.

Two of RFK's biggest supporters and friends were decathlete Rafer Johnson and football player Roosevelt "Rosie" Grier, who traveled with him as his personal bodyguards. That night Rosie was guarding the senator's wife, Ethel Kennedy, who was pregnant with their eleventh child. I could see him standing behind her as Bobby Kennedy spoke. Unlike President John F. Kennedy, Senator Kennedy did not have protection. In those days, political candidates were not offered protection by the Secret Service.

After winning California's primary, Kennedy was in position to receive the Democratic nomination and face Richard Nixon in the general election. After he finished speaking, Bobby Kennedy jumped from the stage and began making his way through the kitchen of the Ambassador Hotel in Los Angeles. After helping Ethel from the stage, Grier said in an interview with the *AARP Bulletin* that he heard gunfire and ran toward the kitchen, where he saw Sirhan, a twenty-two-year-old Palestinian, waving the gun he had hidden in a rolled-up campaign poster. He shot the senator at close range multiple times, as well as several bystanders. Grier tackled the assassin and grabbed the gun. After Bobby Kennedy was taken to the hospital and Sirhan to jail, Grier, known as a gentle giant, slumped to the floor and cried.

My friends and I, along with the rest of the world, were horrified, reliving the tragedy of 1963. Twelve hours later, Robert F. Kennedy died.

On June 6, 1968, Congress passed PL 90-331, expanding the Secret Service's candidate and nominee protection to include major candidates for president and vice president. Several years later, I would learn that the assassination of Robert F. Kennedy and the expanded role of the Secret Service may have brought the need for female agents to the forefront.

Some theorized that if a female agent had been assigned to protect a very pregnant Mrs. Kennedy, Rosie Grier and Rafer Johnson would have been free to stay with Bobby Kennedy and protect him. A female agent assigned to women or children could stay close in private spaces not traditionally appropriate for men, such as restrooms, dressing rooms, and the like. In addition, it is reported that the leadership of the Secret Service believed that adding female agents to its protective and investigative cadre would provide additional resources to support the ever-expanding job of the agency's far-reaching protective responsibility.

On August 8, 1969, President Richard Nixon had a hand in opening the door for women in federal law enforcement, and therefore in the hiring of female Secret Service agents, when he signed Executive Order 11478, Equal Employment Opportunity in the Federal Government. Section 1 states:

> It is the policy of the Government of the United States to provide equal opportunity in Federal employment for all persons, to prohibit discrimination in employment because of race, color, religion, sex, national origin, handicap, or age, and to promote the full realization of equal employment opportunity through a continuing affirmative program in each executive department and agency. This policy of equal opportunity applies to and must be an integral part of every aspect of personnel policy and practice in the employment, development, advancement, and treatment of civilian employees of the Federal Government.

In short, women could be, and should be, hired for all federal positions, including as Secret Service agents. Some thought President Nixon was extending an olive branch to the women's movement. I prefer to think he realized that diversity inclusion was a smart move.

As I was wrapping up a turbulent senior year, both the Vietnam War and the antiwar movement were escalating. Sit-ins by demonstrators temporarily shut down many of the country's colleges and universities. Police would drag the activists' self-imposed limp bodies to jail or disperse the groups with tear gas grenades. Despite their efforts, demands to end the war were not met.

The University of Colorado had its own protests. At one point, there was a movement spearheaded by Students for a Democratic Society, better known as SDS, to rename the Glenn Miller Ballroom the Karl Marx Ballroom. It failed. Conflict among students on campus was the norm. Everyday students like me trying to go to class and graduate were caught in the middle.

Instead, the war in Vietnam ramped up. Between 1965 and 1972 the draft provided 2.2 million service members to the military. President

Richard Nixon issued an executive order prescribing regulations for random selection in 1969. So on an ordinary Monday with little drama or gnashing of teeth, a group of us at CU sat in the rec room watching the only television in the Gamma Phi Beta house. By law, women were not eligible for the draft, but that evening, an estimated 850,000 young men were issued their fate.

After announcing that the trajectory of nearly one million young men's lives was to be dramatically altered, CBS went back to its regularly scheduled programming. We turned off the TV and went to bed, remarkably calm about the whole matter.

Watching protests and drafts on television and reading about legislation changes and body counts in the papers kept me overaware of, but somehow removed from, the horrors of the late 1960s. By 1969, when I graduated college, America was still standing—after a near nuclear war with Russia, missiles pointing at us in Cuba, the three assassinations of JFK, Martin Luther King, and RFK, an unpopular war, the draft, the pill, and thousands of my generation calling for change.

I was right in the middle, a little bit liberal and a little bit politically conservative. I had worn the "T-shirt" of a nonmilitant conservative in college but had a gut feeling that I wanted to be part of the change that was going on. I listened to the call to action from President Kennedy when he said, "We choose to go to the moon because it's hard . . . not because it is easy." Obviously a trip worth taking.

As I neared completion of my elementary education degree, I could never have fathomed what would happen next.

5

Public Relations

MY FUTURE would have been set if I had simply found a husband, gone home, and taught school. After all, that's what most young women did in those days. Not one to follow the crowd, I continued charting my own course. With no husband in sight, I needed a career.

As graduation approached, I turned to Polly Parish, the dean of women at the University of Colorado. The only thing I knew about Ms. Parish was you didn't want to be called to her office for committing a freshman prank, misbehaving, or being late for compulsory curfew. The girls considered her the "gatekeeper." Yet I had never met her.

It wasn't until I became involved in student government and was president of the Panhellenic Council that I came to know and realize the impact Dean Parish was having on the female students at CU. In 1964, she founded the Women's Center, which assisted women later in life in continuing their education or changing vocation.

During my years at CU, Dean Parish was the one faculty member I found on campus who seemed to have her eye on girls who were searching for paths less traveled. She nominated me to serve on the Colorado governor's Commission on the Status of Women. At the time, our status wasn't very good. After I graduated she continued working for better opportunities for women by serving as vice chair of the governor's commission. She oversaw sorority life on campus and guided me through the struggles of dwindling membership. She encouraged me to get out there in front of people, and her self-assured posture inspired me.

Dean Parish's educational honors included Kappa Delta Pi, Phi Beta Kappa, and Mortar Board. She was also a member of Kappa Alpha Theta sorority, but she never told me that. Ultimately, Dean Polly Parish held multiple positions of leadership at CU, earning her the prestigious Stearns Award when she retired.

Turns out there were other things she never told me. When World War II came along, Dean Parish wanted to serve her country and had the distinction of being in the second Navy WAVES class. WAVES was an acronym for Women Accepted for Volunteer Emergency Service. Established in 1942 during World War II, the military unit was the US Navy's corps of female members, with more than one hundred thousand women serving in a wide variety of capacities, ranging from performing essential clerical duties to serving as instructors for male pilots in training. After leaving the Navy WAVES, Dean Parish worked for the US Civil Service in its Naval District Program. Maybe that's why she secretly understood my wanderlust to hit the ground running in Washington.

Dean Parish was an advocate for women no matter how complicated or simple the task. She worked quietly and diligently over decades for small and large change. Dean Parish made the call that changed the direction of my life.

With graduation approaching, I had my sights set on Washington, DC. That's where the action was, so that's where I wanted to be. I sat in Dean Parish's office as she called Republican Colorado congressman Donald Brotzman.

"Yes, Kathryn Clark, that's right," she stated. "I assure you she's the staff assistant you need."

I was amazed. I could not believe she would do that. Just pick up the phone and call a congressman? I didn't realize women *could* do that. She took the bull by the horns, asked the question on my behalf, and changed my life. We should all do that for someone else when we can.

She nodded her head a bit, murmured a few "mmm hmms," and as she smiled, I heard Congressman Brotzman say, "I will give her a call."

A split second later he continued, "Oh, by the way, can she type?"

My heart sank. I had learned that a woman admitting she could type was the kiss of death for her career aspirations. "Secretary for Life," or SFL, would be emblazoned on my forehead. If I were smart enough, I might be promoted to "Executive Secretary," which meant I would run the company *and* type the letters—all for a secretary's pay.

Dean Parish covered the receiver with her hand, half mouthing, half whispering, "You can type, right?"

My head started nodding in the affirmative. Desperate measures were required to get my foot in the door.

Dean Parish smiled and answered the congressman as I nervously pulled at a loose thread on my skirt. Getting to DC was the goal, and if typing a good letter would be necessary, then that was okay.

Unfortunately, Brotzman's staff still hadn't reached out by the time I graduated. With few options, I took a job as a secretary for a geeky-looking group of men who were working at the Alpha Phi house for the summer. They wore thick glasses and plaid shirts with pocket protectors and sat in meetings all day scratching chalk symbols on old blackboards. Turns out they were physicists with some connection to the CIA as part of a "think tank." They became my friends.

Their supervisor suggested I might be a good agent and flew me to Washington for an interview. I was thrilled. They paid for the ticket, and, most importantly, I was able to squeeze in a stop at Congressman Brotzman's office.

As I walked into the congressman's office for our first meeting, he was sitting in a big blue leather chair with brass tacks around the edges. I'd come to learn that all the congressional offices look the same. The congressman was an imposing, good-looking man. My eyes scanned the room. Pictures covered the wall. I focused on a signed photo with President Nixon and the congressman.

"Ms. Clark," the congressman said, interrupting my thoughts. "What do you want to do?"

"I want to go into public relations," I stated simply, not sure what else to say. Public relations was the pat answer for women of the times.

He chuckled, lowered his eyes, and said, "Kathryn, everybody wants to go into public relations. Now let's figure out what you can do here."

We chatted a bit more, and I listened intently.

"We do have an opening—a military caseworker position," he said. "You'll have to be an independent thinker and answer the requests on my behalf. And, you'll have to type your own responses."

Now it was my turn to chuckle softly.

"I can manage that," I said.

Even though I went to the interview with the CIA, I accepted the congressional job as a military caseworker.

Two weeks later, I threw my purse down in the passenger seat of my ice blue '69 VW bug and closed my eyes. I breathed in deeply, my heart racing, and a laugh escaped my lips. "Washington, DC, here I come," I said.

I threw the stick shift into first gear and started the 1,600-mile trek to my new home. I'd done it. I was doing it!

When I pushed in the clutch, I could see the road through a hole in the floor. There were no seatbelts, no air conditioning, no GPS. I was a twenty-two-year-old woman, alone, following a paper road map purchased from a gas station. As I belted out the lyrics to every song that crooned out of my crackling radio, I repeatedly saved my map from escaping through the open windows.

With no idea what was in store for me, I was terrified, but with that fear came an exhilaration and a curiosity that kept me moving forward. Flooring the accelerator of my little VW bug, I could do ninety miles an hour going downhill and made it to my new home within twenty-four hours.

Me, age six.

My father, Lealand Clark, on a hunting trip in the Colorado mountains.

Me dressed as Betsy Ross during the Strawberry Days Parade in Pleasant Grove, Utah.

I competed for the Centennial High School Girl's Rifle Club, where I ranked as one of the top shots in Colorado and earned the award of Distinguished Marksman, the highest qualification given to a junior by the National Rifle Association.

I was one of the first girls selected for the National Junior Ski Patrol at Monarch Pass Ski Area in Gunnison, Colorado, during my sophomore year in high school.

SKI PATROL—Kathy Clark, a Centennial High School senior, is the only girl on the Monarch Pass Ski Area's Junior Ski Patrol. She checks the contents of her first-aid kit, which she wears whenever skiing at the area. The daughter of Mr. and Mrs. L. A. Clark, 2326 DeSoto, she has been skiing for seven years. Kathy also is a member of the Pueblo Tennis Club, on the girls' Rifle Team at Centennial and an accomplished violinist. She has a trophy case filled with awards she has earned in tennis and rifle matches. A member of the National Honor Society, Kathy plans to major in history at the University of Utah after she is graduated from Centennial. She spent last summer traveling in Europe.

Love of Competition Spurs Kathy Clark's Sports Life

By LOU ENGEL

A local newspaper, the *Pueblo Star-Journal*, took note of my sports enthusiasm, success, and ranking as a tennis player, championship rifle shooter, and competitive skier at seventeen years old in June 1965.

A deep love for competition has brought many awards to a 1965 Centennial High School graduate.

High ranking as a tennis player, a Colorado Rifle Association championship and membership in the Monarch Junior Ski Patrol are a few of the honors 17-year-old Kathy Clark has achieved.

Kathy was a member of the Centennial girls rifle team for three years, has been a member of the Pueblo Tennis Club since 1961 and a member of the Monarch Junior Ski Patrol since 1962. She also was a member of the Centennial Racing Club that competed in a ski meet at Winter Park last winter to become the first Pueblo high school to compete in an organized ski event.

These many and varied sports activities apparently have not distracted Kathy from her studies. She stood 38th in the 1965 Centennial graduating class of 509 students. She also was a member of the National Honor Society.

Family Interest in Guns

Kathy became interested in marksmanship because her father and older brother did a lot of deer hunting while she was growing up at Pleasant Grove, Utah.

She joined the rifle team in her sophomore year at Centennial. Kathy was No. 3 in the state last year and her Centennial team placed fourth in the National Rifle Association Junior Championships.

Kathy started playing tennis while visiting her sister and brother-in-law, Dr. and Mrs. Curtis Reemsnyder, in Germany during the summer of 1961.

High Tennis Rankings

Kathy joined the Pueblo Tennis Club on her return from Europe and has been competing in tournaments since that time. In the Southern Colorado Tennis

Kathy Clark
... keen enthusiast for sports

The Intermountain Tennis Association ranks Kathy fifth in women's 18-and-under singles and rates her and Miss Dunley fifth in women's 18-and-under doubles.

President of Ski Club

Kathy's interest in skiing started when she became a member of the Freed Junior High School Ski Club. She was elected president of the club while in the ninth grade.

She became a member of the Monarch Junior Ski Patrol in 1962 and plans to take a test and to become a member of the Ski...

summer and play as much tennis as possible.

Her plans are to return to Colorado to work for a degree in political science and a minor in recreation at the University of Colorado.

Kathy also plans to continue rifle shooting and tennis playing as well as joining a ski racing club.

I was the only woman from Pueblo to be asked to play on a select-only team to compete in matches around the state.

My parents, Lealand and
Ellna Clark, joined me
at the Gamma Phi Beta
house at the University of
Colorado Boulder during
Parents' Day Weekend.

Me (right) with my boss,
Republican Colorado
congressman Donald G.
Brotzman, and his daughter
at a Capitol Hill event.

Working as a military caseworker at the Congressional Office Building.

6

Secret Service on Line Two

NOT KNOWING exactly what I'd gotten myself into, I soon learned that being a military caseworker was more far challenging than I had imagined. Each day, I would walk down the marble halls of the Congressional Office Building to find stacks of letters from men in the military and their families asking for help from their congressman.

Families would request that the congressman use his contacts as an ombudsman with the Military Liaison Office to arrange special leave for a family emergency or intervene if a service member had been abused by a senior officer. My job was to read all the letters, determine which ones deserved the congressman's attention, and do what I could to fix the problem. "You've got to be my eyes and ears, Kathryn," the congressman would remind me. I would thoroughly research the complaints and write up any letter necessary to take action, and he would either sign it or not.

"Oh my gosh," I mumbled under my breath. "How am I, at twenty-two, to know if it is a distraught mother or a guy who has really been abused by the military?" But I'd made it this far and I was going to figure it out. So off I went to my big desk.

It was in a tiny room with high ceilings and a slight view of the flag flying in front of the Capitol. It was cramped with five other large government-looking desks. Behind each sat a smart young college graduate working as an aide of some sort. The guy sitting across from me, Asher

Schmidt, was the congressman's legislative assistant. It was his job to review all the bills and inform the congressman on how to vote. Asher was a funny guy.

I kept a plant on my desk, and once a week he'd say, "Yeah. Girls always have plants on their desk. They don't live; plants die. I don't know why you go to the trouble."

"Because I want to and because it's pretty," I'd retort without looking up from my files.

We didn't disagree just about my greenery—we disagreed on the war. By the time I graduated, I was questioning our actions in North Vietnam, but he was all in favor of ridding the world of communism through any means necessary. One afternoon as we discussed the bombings that were going on in North Vietnam, I continuously threw paper clips at him. He was flirting with me and I was flirting back. He was single and attractive, and although we disagreed on just about everything, I savored the competition and the challenge. Mid paper clip toss, he turned around with his telephone directory in hand, one of the big purple kind that was nearly six inches thick, and heaved it at me. As it hit my desk, with impeccable precision, my plant and stacks of letters went flying. Indignantly, he crossed his arms. "That, my dear, is a lesson in massive retaliation."

"Now you've done it," I said as I picked up my plant.

"I told you it would die," he responded with zero remorse.

We both returned to our work, silent for the remainder of the day. Being a military caseworker was far more challenging than I had imagined, and not just because of my office squabbles.

I remember a request from a heartbroken mother whose son had been killed in Vietnam and was to be buried in Arlington Cemetery. He had a rather long, formal name but had always gone by "Chip." The army by regulation would not allow his nickname to be used on his headstone.

"No one will know who he is," she sobbed into the telephone.

"I don't think this is right," I told Congressman Brotzman.

"I don't either," he said. "Let's see if we can get that changed, Kathy."

It wasn't easy, but we did it. In the end, I typed the official letter to Chip's mother, telling her that her request had been approved and the congressman had signed it. Yes, I typed my own letters, but I was making a difference in people's lives, one military mom, veteran, or soldier at a time.

When I worked for Congressman Brotzman, I came to realize how learning to type on that clunky thirty-pound manual Royal typewriter in high school had been a game changer. Banging away on those stubborn black keys, practicing my secretarial skills to the tune of "Now is the time for all good men to come to the aid of their country," changed my life. In time, I was able to add "women" to the equation. Skill-wise, the more you collect the better.

I responded to as many letters as I could. Some were asking for reprieves from prison sentences, others for permission to come home to attend a funeral, others for early discharge. I did my best to fight for as many requests as I could. And in the process, I learned that congressmen have a lot more power than I was aware. They have significant pull in the government and do a lot more when you ask them. So I suppose that is my public service announcement: if you call your congressman, you can get through to one of his or her staff members and ignite change.

The congressman's staff was intelligent and responsible for many of the decisions he made. Many of these people had aspirations for elected office themselves. This led to our office being a political mosh pit, and most of the aides were conservatives, meaning they supported the war. Walter Cobb, an older, more pompous aide, was a vehement supporter of the military involvement of the United States in Vietnam. He was one of those guys who was "always right," at least in his own brain. There were a lot of guys like that on the Hill. If you asked Walter why we were in Vietnam he would always say, "We are there for our own safety, and for the sake of democracy. If we don't stop the communists in Vietnam, they will be walking up the steps and serving you coffee in the morning."

The specific occupation and location changed, but the basic gist was that the communists would end up on Capitol Hill.

"From all the way in Vietnam?" I'd poke.

"Absolutely," he'd declare.

After a few months working for Congressman Brotzman, a friend I worked with on the Hill told me over lunch that the government was hiring female bodyguards for the first family, specifically Tricia Nixon, daughter of President Richard Nixon.

Between bites of her tuna sandwich, my friend said, "I would be scared to do that, and furthermore, I don't know how to shoot a gun."

I sat in silence, my brain spinning. "Really?" I finally mustered. "I can."

"No you can't!" she laughed, spewing tuna all over her plate.

"Yes I can!" I said emphatically. "My dad taught me and I was on the rifle team in high school. I think I could be good at protecting the first family."

The more we talked, the more enthralled I became. If I got that job, I would have a chance to serve my country, make the world a safer place, work at the White House, and maybe travel on Air Force One with the first family. My mind reverted to the assassination of President Kennedy. I remembered Clint Hill, the man who had saved Mrs. Kennedy on the back of the limo. At the time, I hadn't realized he was a US Secret Service agent, but I had never forgotten how brave he was that day. To protect and serve would be an honor and a remarkable experience.

"Where do you apply?" I asked.

"The Secret Service," she stated.

I submitted my application and held my breath. Several months passed. Things rarely move quickly in Washington.

Then one afternoon, work was slow in the office and we were planning the roster for our softball game against Senator Gordon Allott's office. Conversations from desk to desk turned to the ugly protests over the weekend at the Washington Monument. We couldn't believe that people were spitting on Vietnam veterans. Opinions floated like black clouds around the high ceilings of the large room that housed six staffers. The receptionist called my name through the door. "Hey, Kathy," she said. "Secret Service on line two for you."

The room silenced.

One of the guys chortled and said, "Hey, Clark. Were you protesting this weekend?"

"Shush," I mouthed, picking up the receiver. I had finally gotten the call.

"Hello," I said.

"I am calling for the assistant director of the United States Secret Service, Clinton Hill. He would like to meet with you," the voice on the other end said.

Special Agent Clinton Hill? I had a mental gasp. *The* Clint Hill?

His assistant instructed me to come to Assistant Director Hill's office at Secret Service Headquarters near the Old Executive Office Building the following week for an interview. I used one of my four vacation days, took a cab, and arrived early. I had no idea what to wear to interview to be a special agent. Oh well, I didn't believe the typing thing would be on the table this time.

It was a gray understated building and Clint Hill was an understated man dressed in a gray suit with a white shirt and blue tie. He wore his hero status with little fanfare. There was a serious and melancholy manner about him. As I recall, his eyes were gray blue and could look right through you. In this case, they didn't. He shook my hand and ushered me into his office with a kindness I didn't expect.

The flags of the United States and the Secret Service stood on either side of his desk. Most offices on the Hill were bedecked with signed photographs of important and powerful people. As I recall, Mr. Hill's walls were covered with photos of presidents of the United States and leaders of the free world. His office was impressive yet serious and quiet, with no reference to that fateful day in Dallas. I feel certain there must have been a signed photograph of Jacqueline Kennedy somewhere, but I can't say I saw it.

I would learn he had served many presidents, and the entire Secret Service was regrouping; change was underway. One of things they were considering was hiring women to fill positions as special agents, which was a far more complicated process than I had realized. It would change the history of the agency, and Assistant Director Hill, who was in charge of the protection division, didn't take it lightly.

In all honesty, when I walked into Assistant Director Hill's office I really wasn't exactly sure what the Secret Service did—and I asked him. It wasn't a short answer. The mission was much broader than I realized.

Originally, the Secret Service was established in 1865 under the Department of the Treasury with responsibility to investigate the counterfeiting of US currency, which was rampant following the American Civil War. The agency then evolved into the United States' first domestic intelligence and counterintelligence agency.

Most noticeable, the Secret Service ensures the safety of the president of the United States, the vice president, their immediate families, former presidents, their spouses, and their minor children under the age of sixteen, which includes the children of slain president John F. Kennedy. Major presidential and vice presidential candidates and their spouses as well as foreign heads of state had also recently been added to the protection list.

The Secret Service also provides physical security for the White House complex, the neighboring Treasury Department Building, the vice president's residence, and all foreign diplomatic missions in Washington, DC. The mission includes protective operations to coordinate personnel and logistics with state and local law enforcement, protective advances to conduct site and venue assessments for protectees, and protective intelligence to investigate all manner of threats made against protectees. The organization also safeguards the payment and financial systems of the United States.

Since 2003, the federal law enforcement agency has lived under the Department of Homeland Security. It investigates a wide range of financial and electronic-based crimes. Financial investigations include counterfeit US currency, bank and financial institution fraud, mail fraud, wire fraud, illicit financing operations, and major conspiracies. Electronic investigations include cybercrime, network intrusions, identity theft, access device fraud, credit card fraud, and intellectual property crimes. The Secret Service also helps investigate and combat terrorism on a national and international scale, seeks to reduce and eliminate drug trafficking in critical regions of the United States, and investigates missing and exploited children.

Assistant Director Hill explained the job of protection and we talked about the role the Secret Service played in counterfeit operations protecting US currency. Dangerous undercover work would also be involved. Most importantly, he made it clear that before the interview process moved any further I needed to examine my commitment to "protect and serve," even if it came to giving my own life. I assured him I understood. This was my chance to serve my country; I was willing and able to do whatever the job entailed.

According to Mr. Hill, the Secret Service was the first federal law enforcement agency to recruit women. Most of the applicants were women who had served in law enforcement, many in the DC Police Department. Although I was deficient in that particular area, I did bring an eclectic and unusual skill set. I hoped that would count in the selection process.

During my interview, Mr. Hill asked me the typical questions about my background—where I grew up, where I went to college, what I studied. When I told him elementary education, he didn't blink. I was afraid he would. What interested him was that I was a sharpshooter, skier, equestrian, and tennis player. I could speak German fairly well and was great with children. Interestingly, it was those random things I loved to do and brought to the table that counted in the end. Even my public relations skills from working on the Hill seemed to serve a purpose.

One specific question sticks in my mind to this day. "If you were protecting the first lady and she told you to stay behind—that she didn't need your services, what would you do?" he asked.

I pondered for a moment and said, "No matter who she is—if it is my job to protect her, I can't do it staying behind. I suppose I would tell her that, in an appropriate yet respectful manner."

Coach Wentworth's words about gumption entered my brain when I thought about this scenario. Perhaps that, too, would come in handy in this job.

At the conclusion of my interview, it became clear that Mr. Hill was one of the men of the United States Secret Service who would without hesitation support hiring women. He would continue to be one of our biggest advocates over the years.

7

Trying Us On for Size

PHYLLIS Shantz, Laurie Anderson, Sue Ann Baker, Holly Hufschmidt, and yours truly—we have gone down in history as the first women to risk their lives in the Secret Service. We were, in fact, a risk for the Secret Service itself. President Nixon's Executive Order for Equal Employment Opportunity in the Federal Government suggested that a door might open for us; the Secret Service was the first federal law enforcement agency to open that door. Being the first is always difficult and comes with some risk, but I suppose that is necessary for progress to be made.

First proposed by the National Woman's Party in 1923, the Equal Rights Amendment was to provide for the legal equality of the sexes and prohibit discrimination on the basis of sex. Yet "women need not apply" or "no women allowed" were the pat answers to most questions when it came to jobs, credit, or civil rights. Still today, I am surprised at how relatively complacent so many women were about it, accepting "that's just the way it is."

Fifty years ago, the rowdy ones, the women who called themselves "women's libbers," dared to shout about it and demonstrated in the streets, calling for equal rights and opportunities across the board.

On March 22, 1972, the Equal Rights Amendment was passed by the US Senate and sent to the states for ratification. Many Americans assume the United States has gender-equality rules. After all, the Civil Rights Act, Title IX, and the Equal Pay Act all offer protections against discrimination. But these are pieces of legislation. New laws and Supreme Court rulings can diminish their power.

We continue to have a glass ceiling. The gender pay gap still favors men.

The Secret Service's landmark open-door policy to hire female officers and agents was on the books in 1970, but this historical shift could hardly be celebrated at the time. No one knew how the men already in the agency would receive this change. Although there was an order to accept the new recruits, no one could force positivity or acceptance, and the current agents' attitudes and cooperation were imperative in making this new equation work. As someone once said to me, "You can't legislate morality or civility or acceptance." Working with a colleague with high self-esteem wasn't difficult. Self-importance was a different story. Even today, people who are considered "full of themselves" create roadblocks to the integration of genders, cultures, and religions. Thankfully, those folks were scarce in my case.

What they don't tell you is that when you break that glass ceiling, failure isn't exactly an option.

On September 4, 1970, I received an official letter from Joseph N. Fosta, chief of personnel for the Secret Service, saying that I had been selected. The letter informed me of the details of my appointment. I was to earn $8,500 per annum and should report for duty on October 5, 1970, for sixteen weeks of training.

I'm not quite sure how they picked us, but five women were selected and would become the first class of females hired by the Secret Service. I was thrilled, grateful, and a little terrified of what would come next. That fear, though? That was the adrenaline rush that propelled me and my four cohorts right through our proverbial glass ceiling.

A diverse bunch, we came from all over the country. Phyllis was from New York, Laurie hailed from Jersey City, New Jersey, and Holly and Sue Ann grew up in Milwaukee and Oak Ridge, Tennessee, respectively. These four had served in the DC Metropolitan Police Department and had a better idea of what they were in for. I was the staffer from the Hill with an education degree.

Thankfully I wasn't five foot nothing like Ms. Annie Oakley, because you had to be at least five feet seven with 20/20 vision. The good Lord saw fit to bless me with a whole five feet eight inches and eyes that didn't need glasses to see the cans I was shooting from fence posts or to scan crowds for potential threats to those under my protection. Growing up under the watchful eye of my parents ensured that the exhaustive background investigation would turn up squeaky clean as well.

The tests for strength and agility were tough, but more than doable. I was meant for this role and unknowingly had been preparing for it the last twenty-two years. Nowadays, to be deemed "excellent," the highest qualification of fitness, a woman in her twenties is expected to complete a mile and a half run faster than twelve minutes fifty seconds, do four chin-ups, forty-four sit-ups in one minute, and forty push-ups in a minute. There were no standards when we were going through training. I couldn't do even one pull-up, but I was naturally athletic and ambitious, and I gave the instructors a reason to believe I could become a capable agent.

A physical exam for overall health was also required. The other girls had already taken their exams at the DC Police Department when they were officers. As I was the only one of us without a law enforcement background, the Secret Service sent me to a fire station in Southeast Washington for my physical.

"Name?" the officer checking us in grunted without looking up from his list.

"Clark."

The sound of a female's voice must have knocked him out of his check-marking routine. He looked up abruptly.

"Kathryn," I finished, locking eyes with him and smiling just enough to let him know that yes I was there, and yes I was absolutely where I was supposed to be.

He cleared his throat. "Morning, Miss Clark. Please sign here. Fill this out. And ummm . . ." he stumbled with his words. "We're going to . . . umm . . . need to collect a . . . ummm . . . sample."

With that he looked down and shoved a couple of papers and a plastic cup in my hands. I shuffled down the long station to the restroom. Push-ups I had mentally prepared for. Walking in front of two hundred wannabe civil servants with a cup of my own urine, not so much.

Trying to ignore the impending long walk back, I thought about deserts and dry Utah summers. "Focus," I told myself. Now in the bathroom, I began to try to think of rivers, rainfall, and cold lemonade on a summer day. I finally relaxed enough to get the minimum, eh, uh, sample. Straightening my shoulders, I pressed my lips together and unlocked the door. Here we go.

"There she is!"

"Ow-ow."

Whistles.

Laughter.

"Hey there, pretty thing. You lost?"

More laughter.

More whistles.

Phyllis Shantz's words echoed in my head. "Keep your eyes down. If they don't get a rise out of you, they'll leave you alone."

"At least I know I'm going to pass this part. Are you?" I joked with one of the men, not truly confident enough to look him square in the face. The retort itself shut him up, while also garnering a bit of respect from those standing next to him.

Carrying a urine sample in a cup past a gauntlet of jeering, belligerent young men wasn't fun. But there weren't enough of us who had had to do it to have a protocol in place. And although this was the first time I experienced the bullheaded stupidity of men who had never employed women, it wouldn't be the last time. Phyllis was right. Keeping my emotions in check and my sense of humor intact, I dropped my cup off with all the others and joined the line. I had to earn to my right to be on the team, and if that mean brushing off a little catcalling from boys who didn't know any better, I'd do just that.

Actor Tom Hanks said in the movie *A League of Their Own*, "There's no crying in baseball." I would add—in the same context—there is no crying in the Secret Service. I never cried. Not that day in that Southeast Washington fire station. Not ever.

Not even when we realized that headquarters wanted to "try out" the girls initially before making the leap to the full appointment of women as special agents. Disappointment is an understatement. We had the background, the experience, and the college degrees required of agents, yet it would take nearly a year for that day to come. Was that fair? Probably not. Realistic? Probably so. It was a learning process for all of us. The five of us were the forward observers for women who would follow—or not—depending on how we survived, and the agency's mission was improved because of our presence and performance.

No one knew what to expect, so everyone proceeded with caution. The officers and agents of the service were civil and supportive. At the same time, they kept watch to make sure we were carrying our load. I think that was fair, and I did my best to make sure I did. When our forefathers penned, "All men are created equal," it's interesting they didn't mention women. I suppose it is assumed, but it took a long time for women's equality to move to the forefront of the political debate. In the 1970s women began seriously knocking on doors, asking for equal rights, and applying for equal employment opportunities. A few of those doors began to open—others were knocked down. Each woman who crossed one of those thresholds threatened the status quo.

I saw a *Cathy* cartoon in the *Washington Post* one Sunday afternoon that read, "Women who seek to be equal with men lack ambition." I suppose it was a rallying cry for the liberated women marching in the streets, but it most likely put fear in the hearts of some men. Remarkably, the Secret Service, the oldest and most prestigious law enforcement agency in America, became the first to hire female special agents. That willingness was not only forward thinking, it was courageous, and ultimately it changed history.

They gave women a chance and worked to prepare us for the opportunity. Yes, their actions fell in step with the political march to make equal opportunities for women available, but more importantly they appeared to believe that bringing women into the equation supported their mission. To put it simply, women can do things men can't do and vice versa. We were one of the first experiments in a time of social and political change that continues today.

Today, the most common question I'm asked is how we (the five women) were treated by the men. It's almost as though folks are hoping I will report nothing but conflict and confrontation. I suppose that's more exciting than if I said, "Actually, we got along fine."

And with that point the five women got along fine as well and remain friends today.

That's not to say dropping women into the middle of a male comfort zone was easy. It took more time for some of the men to get used to it than others. Oh sure, there were some jokes, language, and bad attitudes thrown our way, but in my case they were few and far between. I didn't let it get in my way and the men didn't either.

Was it fair that the service took an inordinate amount of time to move us up to special agent status? Looking back, I think it was, even though it was disappointing. Because we were the first women to join the ranks, they were as anxious for us to succeed as we were. While we were in the midst of on-the-job training we were being vetted. Were we strong enough, mindful enough, and good enough to serve with the men? Evidently we were.

In the end, the male agents were accepting and supportive and became my friends. I am proud to have served with them. We were men and women contributing in our own ways—each of us striving to be the best that we could be. I think that's better than just being equals.

8

At Home in the District

MY CAPITOL HILL salary was meager. When I joined the Secret Service, my annual salary of $8,500 was not much higher, so I found myself living on Forty-Fourth Street with Susan Davis and three other women who also worked on the Hill. The house was a classic Georgetown brick brownstone. Five of us shared three bedrooms. Susan found the place and sublet it from a woman at the State Department who was on an overseas assignment. She was an entrepreneur even in those days. Now Susan has her own international company and significant influence in Washington. I always knew she would do something of consequence.

Susan claimed the master bedroom with a large four-poster canopy bed. She was in charge and had a handsome boyfriend. The three newest girls, including Ponce Andres from Colorado and me, shared an upstairs bedroom outfitted with bunks and a single bed along the wall. We also shared a bathroom. Typically, mornings were crazy until I got the job at the White House and had to be there by 6:00 a.m. Then I had the bathroom all to myself. In spite of, or perhaps because of, our close quarters, we became fast friends.

"You're going to carry a gun?" Ponce had asked. "Will you bring it home with you?"

"Of course. I'm on duty twenty-four seven protecting some pretty important people."

The new girls of Forty-Fourth Street weren't wearing "Make Love Not War" T-shirts and certainly wouldn't admit it if they were. Keep in mind, the pill was still fairly new—although some of us had prescriptions to battle acne, or just in case—and no young men I knew carried condoms. It was a big decision to have sex. Some of us made it through college with our virginity intact. Either no one had asked or we were scared to death of getting pregnant. We did, however, get pretty good at making out while trying to save our reputations.

For a brief time I dated Walter, an arrogant guy I had worked with on Capitol Hill. He thought I was crazy to have left the congressman's office, and he liked to tease me about how tough I was. One night at a party, he started his typical banter. "Kathy Clark thinks she is pretty tough," he said, laughing.

I had had enough and slipped my cuffs out of my bag. Within seconds I had handcuffed him to his chair. Everyone thought it was funny, including Walter, until I realized I didn't have the key. It took two hours to retrieve it from my apartment and free him.

He never asked me out again. I really don't blame him.

Ponce and I had a couple of cute guys from Colorado who also worked on the Hill that became our friends and weekend pals. I wouldn't say they were our "boyfriends," but we hung out together at our house on Forty-Fourth Street, cooked dinner, played the Carpenters and Joan Baez on the stereo, and drank Mateus, a popular brand of Portuguese sweet wine. We kept the bottles and stuck multicolored candles into them. As they burned down, we pushed one on top of the other and they dripped down the sides, making popular candle holders that most everyone had in their apartments.

I don't recall going to clubs much but Washington weekends were always fun, with multiple things to do that didn't cost much. Concerts on the banks of the Potomac were always fun. We did more of that kind of thing before I joined the service. After that I was rarely home.

What I loved to do—with or without friends—was take a bus down M Street to the National Mall to visit the National Portrait Gallery. I would spend all Sunday afternoon wandering the cavernous halls. One of my favorite exhibitions was a study of women in hats by an American artist, Mary Cassatt, who later lived in France. A print of a painting I loved hangs in my home today—a little girl with soulful eyes, probably seven years old and dressed in what looked to me like a French peasant dress. She was wearing a feed sack–colored knee-length smock covering a simple white T-shirt that peeked out and covered her little girl arms just above the elbow.

But what caught my attention was the little girl's oversized wide-brimmed straw hat, tied with a big black-and-white bow. There was a message in the way the bow was tied, as if her mother had plopped the hat on her head and said, "There . . . now you look like somebody. Go out into the world and make something of your life. Look like you belong." The rumpled bow appeared to be an afterthought, though.

I'm not sure why the image touched me, but it still does. Perhaps that is why I so often mention the "look like you belong" dilemma. I had the basics when I arrived at the Secret Service, but as an agent it often took more than a floppy hat and a big bow to look like I blended in.

9

Bang . . . You're Dead!

AT THE TIME, bringing women into the Secret Service was historic. But the agency did not seem to be fully prepared for the changes necessary to add the opposite sex into the mix. Many of the logistics had yet to be worked out.

My general information letter for recruit training—addressed to Mr. Clark, mind you—said we were to wear a business suit, dress shirt, coat, and tie, and we were to supply our own gym clothes—gray gym trunks, a gray T-shirt, gym shoes, white athletic socks, an athletic supporter, soap, and a towel. Yes you read that correctly, an *athletic supporter*, and they were not talking about a sports bra. I'm not sure how long it took them to draft a second letter geared more toward females, but it wasn't during my tenure.

For the first few months, I was alone in the Executive Protective Service (EPS) training program because the rest of the girls had trained with the Washington Police Department. I was elected secretary of my class. Surprise, surprise! I was actually flattered to be elected to anything and was willing to do my part. My courses focused on legal processing, law and courts, community relations, arrest techniques, and police procedures. In addition, we were shown a film on how to deliver a baby in the back of a police car. I was the only woman in a room with fifty men.

The training was fun. I loved driving police cars in high-speed chases, my red lights flashing and sirens blaring while speeding down an abandoned runway and hitting an oil slick that the instructors had put out. You'd momentarily lose control of the car, but it was to teach you to correct your wheels, to slide out of the oil and regain control of the car. I was quite good at it, having grown up in Colorado. The trick is to turn your wheels in the direction of the slide. To me that was an adrenaline rush. For a while, my training class called me "Slick" because I loved going fast. Even today, I love to go to parking lots, race around a bit, and hear the sound of squealing tires.

Weapons training came easily as well; I was a good shot. Night shooting was a little more complicated. I learned to hold a flashlight in my left hand away from my body and my gun in my right hand. This was meant to confuse a perpetrator and keep him from shooting at the light and killing me.

During law enforcement training, they assigned us to various locations, sometimes parks or an old beat-up house at a training facility. The house was staged to look like an actual home. The bedroom had a real bed, sheets, pillows, and more. For one particular session, they took one of our girls and put her in the bed.

Another agent and I were supposed to go in and make the arrest. "Federal agent, don't move or I'll shoot," I said, drawing my gun outside the bedroom door.

Supposedly, arresting your suspect in bed was not an unusual situation. Holly, my fellow agent who'd been selected as our temporary perp, started screaming. It was mostly bad language followed by more bad language, so I'll leave that to your imagination.

My partner kicked in the door, and I could see Holly with the sheet up around her neck. With guns pointed at her, she screamed, "Get out of here, you pig. I'm naked! I'm naked!"

"Holly Hufschmidt, you're no more naked than I am," I yelled. "Get your ass out of there."

We were friends, and we laughed as I cuffed her and pushed her out of the training house.

Often, the streets were filled with tear gas during the many demonstrations in the 1970s. We had to learn how to handle these incidents should we find ourselves caught in them. To prepare, we put on gas masks and were herded into an old army tent filled with tear gas; we were then told to remove our masks and count to twenty. Our eyes burned and watered, and our throats closed. I learned that rubbing my face made it worse.

The only thing I could do was get out of there and run. At some point, an industrial-size fan would blow the gas away.

One of the funniest parts of police training was having to direct traffic. At the corner of Pennsylvania Avenue, they put out an apple crate for me to stand on.

I had to position a metal whistle in my mouth so that it wouldn't fall out while I used both hands to direct the cars. I was instructed to blow three sharp blasts to stop the oncoming traffic. Once all the cars were halted, I'd motion the other direction to go.

When I got off the box, the rest of my training class was there to greet me. By this point, they were very accepting of me. They gathered around and one guy asked, "What's it like out there?"

I'd played the violin in school, and I sensed a comparable musicality and structure to directing traffic. "It's like directing a band or orchestra, just get a rhythm. You know, put your hand out, blow the whistle, stop the rest of them. Make it fun, like you're directing a band."

"Oh, I get it, so there's a timing to it."

"Exactly."

So there we were—thirty guys and me playing traffic cop.

One of the most important things the Secret Service taught us was to question everything, to trust our intuition, and to live by this mantra: if it doesn't look right, it probably isn't. One night during an outdoor exercise in the National Arboretum, a huge park we often used for training, I was paired with a male classmate. We were chasing a car driven by instructors at speeds over one hundred miles per hour. With our lights flashing and sirens blaring, we were supposed to overtake the instructors (the "bad guys"), pull them over, and make arrests. We were practically on their bumper when they slowed and suddenly stopped.

My partner and I drew our guns, screaming, "Secret Service! Get out of the car! Drop your weapons! On the ground!"

We started to exit our vehicle when suddenly the car took off again. We were in hot pursuit a second time, tires squealing and throwing gravel, when within a hundred yards or so, they stopped again and threw their guns out the windows. We pulled our weapons and slid out of the car, crouching behind our open car doors.

"Secret Service! You are under arrest!" I screamed again. "Exit the vehicle!" I demanded. We thought there were four men in the car but weren't sure. Four men gingerly exited the vehicle with their hands up.

"Did you count how many were in the car?" I yelled at my partner.

"No," he said, breathing heavily. "Couldn't see inside. You?"

I shook my head no. Things had suddenly gotten quiet. The four men stood with their hands up in the air, illuminated by our glaring headlights.

"Too easy," he said, looking worried.

"Right," I responded as I tried desperately to scan the scene in front of me. I was so focused that I didn't hear the footsteps behind me.

Then I felt the cold steel muzzle of a gun against my neck.

"Bang . . . you're dead," said the fifth instructor in a low, almost inaudible tone that I heard loud and clear. He had rolled out of the car after the brief stop and got the drop on me when their car finally came to a halt.

I've never forgotten that night and that dead, cold feeling. It was instrumental in my training, and it changed the way I looked at things. It was another lesson in the vanilla factor. Bottom line—if it doesn't look, feel, or smell right, it probably isn't.

10

Shots Fired

"ONE FOOT on the brake, Agent Clark," Agent Smith, my instructor, breathed to my right. "One on the accelerator."

It was a good thing he was breathing because I wasn't. This was the first time I'd been truly scared during a training exercise. I had my left foot on the brake and my right foot on the accelerator of the "follow-up car" for the presidential limousine. Normal people did not drive like this. Learning to drive in Colorado, I'd been normal and had used my right foot for both stopping and going. But now I was a special agent. We had to be ready to stop instantly without any warning.

"How many feet you keepin' between your car and the limo?" Agent Smith asked.

"Two. So no other car can get in between the follow-up car and the limo, sir."

"Good. Now step on it."

And I did. I brought the car up to eighty-seven miles per hour and did as instructed, staying slightly to the left of the back of the limo, not even two feet from the rear bumper of the car I was trailing.

"What do I do if the limo stops?" I asked, knowing the answer. Why does the mouth begin working before the brain tells it to stop? My brain should really stop me from asking stupid questions.

Agent Smith raised his caterpillar eyebrows at me.

"Right," I nodded. "Be on your toes. Be quick. No room for error."

Frustrated that my thinking out loud would be perceived as uncertainty, I narrowed my vision and focused on the car in front of me. There would be no motorcade intervention on my watch.

Other vehicular training exercises were less stressful, but just as exhilarating. We practiced running alongside the massive black presidential limousine; let the record show, we kept up with the men. Re-creating history, we trained to carry out Clint Hill's dauntless leap onto the back of President Kennedy's limousine should the need arise. Having watched the act on television and interviewed with Assistant Director Hill himself to be selected as a Secret Service agent, I found it a little unnerving to follow in his footsteps. And unfortunately, I couldn't. But neither could a single one of the men. We couldn't make the jump Agent Hill had executed on the day Kennedy was assassinated. Instead of being ashamed, we were in awe of him. Adrenaline and the call of duty allow the mind and body to perform powerful feats.

That is what is, and was, expected of a special agent. While working alongside the men—oftentimes as the only woman—I learned to protect, and to make life-altering split-second decisions. The training was ongoing. The scrutiny was severe. We were afforded no mistakes, partially because we were dealing with gender barriers in unknown territory during tumultuous times, and in part because we were reviewed upon our reliability and effectiveness when it came down to protecting the likes of President Richard Nixon, Henry Kissinger, Indira Gandhi, Prime Minister Golda Meir, and the Princess of Spain. Man or woman, you swore to protect the aforementioned, along with your fellow agents. You always had your partner's back and your partner had yours.

Having your partner's back and protecting the most influential dignitaries in the world required shooting straighter than Annie Oakley herself. To make sure we were capable, we had to "qualify" every two to four weeks. Qualifying meant shooting top scores with standard-issue .357 Magnum revolvers in the dank shooting range in the subbasement of the Treasury Building.

The Treasury Building took up the corner of Fifteenth Street and Pennsylvania Avenue. With its massive granite structure and gigantic Corinthian pillars, it covered a two-block area. The building housed the entire Department of the Treasury, and since the initial, formative purpose of the Secret Service was to protect the currency of the United States after the Civil War, it made sense that our shooting range was hidden beneath it.

To get there from the White House, I walked along a "secret" underground, buttercup-yellow concrete tunnel that zigzagged the length of three football fields (782 feet) from the subbasement of the East Wing. The tunnel was built in 1941 to evacuate then-President Roosevelt to secure vaults in the Treasury Building in the event of an emergency. The path felt cold and clandestine, brightly lit but clammy. When you passed another there was a nod—an acknowledgment of the path, not the destination. No one ever spoke. As my heels clicked on the painted gray concrete floors, I felt a rush of what I called Potomac Fever. It was a walk I did regularly, yet some days the routine was lost in the history. That walk was part of what seemed like a make-believe journey I was taking.

Checking my credentials, a Secret Service instructor allowed me to push open the heavy door that opened to a long, dark room simply called the range. It was well lit at the far end where three-by-four-foot paper targets hung in front of a bunker of sandbags.

As I entered the range, I thought about this venerated space where the likes of Special Agents Clint Hill and Jerry Parr had trained. I was prepared to load my weapon with deadly hollow-point shells and take accurate aim.

Black-and-white images of an armed, full-size man from his suit coat up hung like sheets on an old-fashioned clothesline. I would take my position alongside a line of male agents wearing bulky ear protection and clear protective glasses. The sound was deafening. A thin line of gray smoke from each shot curled toward the ceiling. The exploding gunpowder filled our nostrils with a subtle sulfur smell. Slugs tearing through the chests of the paper targets made a rat-a-tat rhythm, followed by the whir of an electric motor that returned their devastated torsos to the instructor, who, with a nod, would confirm accuracy or not. Amid this cacophony it became clear this was not just a drill—this was serious business. It was no longer a sport I liked to play. This was my job.

Each agent was given a box of shells that sat like eggs in a little red plastic carton. An officer or agent overseeing the "qualifiers" would grab a target off one of the big musty-looking stacks. The room itself was dark like a cave, but the black gunpowder residue that wallpapered all surfaces gave it a more ominous feeling. The target was the size of a man and the image showed him pointing a gun at you—as if that made it easier for us to take the task of tearing him to shreds seriously.

As the instructors stood behind the agents, we shooters would hit a button and our life-size target would zip to the end of the range. I loaded my gun, placing five rounds into my standard-issue revolver. We always left one round empty where the hammer was, as a safety factor.

It was a cacophony of bullets firing, guns opening and clicking closed, targets whizzing backward and forward, paper tearing as the bullet made its deadly impact. The goal was to hit the middle of the chest of the target with precision and speed. It seems ironic that while safely underground, I was the closest I'd ever get to firing at an actual suspect.

If I'd allowed myself to think about it, the repercussions and intent of the training could have been overwhelming. In the Secret Service, you never shoot a warning shot. If you unholster your weapon, you need to be prepared to shoot to protect. If the suspect is running away from you and your protectee, you don't fire, but those decisions are made in a split second. If you aim to protect, you aim to kill. One instructor said you never fire warning shots into the air, because you can never be sure of your surroundings. If you fired through the ceiling, Granny could be on the top floor knitting and you could kill an innocent woman.

Leaving the Treasury Building, I was exhilarated when I made top scores, but relieved that those deadly shells were tearing through only paper, not bone and blood. How is it possible to want to be so good at something you hope you never have to do? It's like training your whole life for a race, but crossing your fingers you never have to run it. I knew one day I might not be shooting at paper targets. I might have to shoot someone with my weapon or take an assassin's round myself. I was ready.

When I was assigned to the foreign dignitary protective detail, Jerry Parr was the special agent in charge. Among those who knew him inside and outside the Secret Service, he was admired as a patient man willing to hear out our troubles, keep confidences, and talk through the hills and valleys of the job. We talked one afternoon while I sat with him on board Air Force One (aircraft tail number 2600 when it did not have the president on board), flying to California with the Spanish royals.

I asked him how you mentally prepared for the day everything would go south. He smiled and said quietly, "Kathy, you plan for the absolute worst and pray for the best."

That answered my question, and I thought about it every time I qualified at the range.

Ten years later, everything did go south. Jerry Parr was protecting President Reagan during the assassination attempt on his life on March 30, 1981, in Washington, DC. In the aftermath, Parr was celebrated for his cool ability to confront danger and direct a path to safety. He did his job, and along with what was left of the detail, he saved the president's life. He became a mentor, a hero, and a dear friend to me.

"There's a couple of times where truth and training converge, where history and destiny converge," Mr. Parr told the *Washington Post* in 2006. "I thought about that for a long time. It's that moment—either you do it or you don't, either you save him or you don't."

Researching this book, I found an interview on YouTube where Jerry Parr described the day he was protecting President Ronald Reagan and shots rang out. "When President Reagan was about six to seven feet from the door of the car, I heard these shots. I sort of knew what they were. I been waiting for them all of my career, in a way. That's what every agent waits for. The most natural thing to do was get his head down and push him real hard into the car. And I went in on top of him. Shift leader Ray Shadick threw our feet inside and slammed the door shut. I looked out the back window and there were three bodies on the sidewalk. I thought we were clear, but then he started spitting up blood. I looked at it and said, 'I'm taking you to the hospital.' He looked pretty bad. And I asked God to let him live. I got right over his face and said that, 'Lord let him live.'"

Parr's words, "Plan for the worst and pray for the best," came back to me.

11

Tour Guide

IN THE BEGINNING, the five of us were assigned to the Executive Protective Service (EPS) within the Secret Service before we became special agents. With training completed, I reported for duty at 1600 Pennsylvania Avenue. It was 6:00 a.m., just before sunrise—cold and dark—with few people on the street. The Secret Service code name for the White House was "Wedding Cake" because it looked like one. My arrival was anticlimactic and met with little fanfare. When I checked in at the side gate to the East Wing, the officer took my identification and told me to report to the basement command post.

At the command post, an impressive man in a black uniform with the presidential seal over his name badge issued me a new Smith and Wesson .357 Magnum snub-nosed revolver, still in its box, and twelve rounds of hollow-point ammunition. He also gave me a gold executive protective service badge with the number seven stamped on the back. With the popularity of James Bond's agent number 007, I thought it was good sign. Finally, he gave me a black leather commission book complete with a paragraph inside stating I was on a mission for the president of the United States and should be afforded all courtesy and authority accordingly. He also threw in a pair of handcuffs. I made sure there was a key attached and kept it where I could find it.

However, the most exciting thing he issued me was an American Express credit card, which I slid gingerly into my wallet. Even with the enormity of the rest of the gear, the credit card was the biggest of deals. If asked on that day what was in my wallet, all I could have claimed was a Conoco gas credit card on loan from my father. In those days, women could not get a credit card or a loan without a husband or father to cosign. Even then, it was rarely in her own name.

I initialed a lot of paperwork, and the EPS captain smiled and put it all in a cardboard box for me to take home.

During the early days of women in the Secret Service, White House assignments varied. Some were definitely better than others. We all rotated through assignments that included observing maids cleaning the White House offices, standing post on the grounds, and monitoring food deliveries.

Remarkably, my teaching degree and minor in art history from the University of Colorado came in handy. Those days, one of my assignments was as a White House tour guide. The difference between regular tour guides and EPS tour guides was that we carried guns. The public was allowed to walk through velvet-roped lines, getting a glimpse of the "living history" of the presidential family and those who had lived there before them. More in-depth congressional tours had to be arranged through an office on Capitol Hill or with the White House staff. Groups of thirty to fifty people were escorted by armed guards undercover as tour guides, such as yours truly, touring spaces that were within a stone's throw of the Oval Office.

As a "tour guide," my job was to protect the president and first family from harm while entertaining, informing, and controlling the curious visitors touring the presidential home, without letting them know I was armed. Through my earpiece, I was informed of the movements and whereabouts of the president. Often he was only down the hall in the Oval Office as I guided the public through the White House, but that was not for them to know.

Each day, I stood in the middle of the East Room with personal friends of the president or hundreds of unruly schoolchildren, explaining how the oldest object in the White House was the painting of George Washington that hung behind me. When the British burned the White House in 1814, First Lady Dolly Madison cut the canvas from the frame, rolled it up, and took it with her as she escaped. I had watched Mrs. Kennedy guide America through the refurbished White House on a black-and-white television in 1962, but I had never dreamed I would be inside this amazing home giving tours. This was probably the first time I was cognizant that my knowledge about art and American history would serve me well.

I learned to read an audience and tell a good story while on assignment at the White House. Imagine how much fun it was to open the purple rope, walk into the middle of the East Room, a magnificent ballroom that was graced with floor-to-ceiling windows that displayed vistas of Washington flanked by ancient magnolia trees planted by Thomas Jefferson himself, and mesmerize an audience with that story.

On various occasions, I introduced myself to the president's personal guests, foreign heads of state, or the public and told them how President Teddy Roosevelt's children had kept their pony in the same room in which Mrs. Roosevelt had hung her laundry to dry. I explained that President Truman loved to play the piano and would entertain guests on the magnificent Steinway grand piano where he also belted out "Happy Birthday" to First Lady Bess.

I would point to the mammoth chandeliers above. "How do you suppose the White House staff cleans them?" I would ask. No one would ever dare answer.

"Very carefully," I would quip, answering my own question, and off we would go to the Green Room, Blue Room, Red Room, and State Dining Room. Sometimes it got a laugh, sometimes it didn't. But I suppose that's show business, and guiding people around the most famous residence in the world was as close to show business as I'd ever been.

Sometimes, when the first family was not in residence, I gave tours of the private quarters upstairs. The second floor was beautiful. Sunlight streamed through the windows and bounced off the vibrant lemon-yellow walls. Fresh flowers were everywhere. The White House had its own florist and floral shop. Actually, the White House had its own everything.

One afternoon, when I was upstairs waiting for several guests of President Nixon, I peeked into his bathroom. A huge presidential seal was emblazoned on the side of the tub, and at the side hung a telephone, a rare sight in those days. I supposed one of the most powerful men in the world should be accessible anywhere and everywhere.

As I walked past the bathroom, I noticed floppy white boxer shorts folded neatly atop the bathmat, which also boasted the presidential seal. I couldn't help but chuckle. It shouldn't be surprising that our commander in chief had to wear undergarments, the same as everyone else, but I can't say I ever thought about President Jefferson or President Lincoln having his underdrawers folded up on the tub in the White House.

12

History of the House

WHILE WE were assigned to the Executive Protective Service, the girls were sent on details all over the country. Test runs, so to speak. Phyllis preferred criminal counterfeit investigation, as did Laurie Anderson. Denise Ferrenz, the sixth woman to join the Secret Service, and Sue Ann Baker were frequently assigned to Vice President Agnew and his family and worked the McGovern presidential candidate detail.

Holly Hufschmidt worked a lot of protection. She had a great sense of humor and a distinctive voice. We loved to hear her on the radio at the White House.

"Officer Hufschmidt, South Grounds rounds," she would announce. There was no question a woman was on duty, and we were proud of that.

Carrying out my assignment as a tour guide, I worked for Mr. Clem Conger, curator of the White House. Conger oversaw the conservation of the collection of fine art, furniture, and decorative objects used to furnish both the public and private rooms of the White House as an official residence and as an accredited historic house museum. His office was established during the administration of President John F. Kennedy, while First Lady Jacqueline Kennedy oversaw the restoration of the building.

The first curator was Lorraine Waxman Pearce, a decorative arts scholar, who helped Jacqueline Kennedy restore the presidential mansion to its nineteenth-century historic splendor.

Mr. Conger did not work directly with Mrs. Kennedy. He came to the White House at the insistence of President Nixon. It was reported in the *Washington Post* that the Nixons toured the diplomatic reception rooms at the State Department one day in 1969, when Conger was officially deputy chief of protocol. Evidently the president liked what he saw. That same afternoon, he asked him to transfer to the White House.

Conger's stories and background information were legendary. As he showed me around, Conger declared, "Kings, queens, and prime ministers marvel when told these pieces are American. They thought we had no culture."

Besides showcasing eighteenth- and nineteenth-century American style, the antiques also served as conversation pieces when, as Conger put it, "diplomatic language faltered."

A compulsive collector of great stories about the White House, Conger told of a meeting between President Theodore Roosevelt and the Japanese ambassador. The opening chitchat dwelt on the rare American china they were using for tea. Unaccustomed to handling this sort of teacup, the fumbling ambassador dropped his cup and broke it. Roosevelt immediately let his cup fall to the floor as well, muttering, "They do break easily."

That was good protocol, but Conger could not be so casual. "We don't leave many knickknacks lying around," he said, "because even at the most elegant presidential parties, things like ashtrays have a way of disappearing."

So in addition to protecting the first family, I also served to protect American history and the artifacts that preserve our country's legacy. As a young woman, I admired Mrs. Kennedy's resolve to make the White House a "living museum."

"As I recall, prior to the Kennedy years, the historical beauty of the house had not been a priority. Oftentimes, the first lady's personal belongings were used to furnish the president's house," Conger said.

Prior to its refurbishment, many of the historical pieces and antiques of the White House were scattered among warehouses and storage units throughout the district. "Mrs. Kennedy literally pulled on her capri pants and Ked sneakers and started prowling basements, attics, and federal storage facilities looking for anything of historical and artistic merit to bring the White House back to its glory days," he explained. One afternoon in the Blue Room, he pointed to a large gilded buffet near me. "That piece was downstairs in the carpenter's shop as a worktable—one step from the trash pile," he said. Mrs. Kennedy recognized something about the rickety old bench and realized its historic significance. Conger concluded, "She brought it back upstairs and back to life."

Looking out the window to the Washington Monument and Jefferson Memorial across the South Grounds, Conger spoke of a time when President Kennedy had been hosting a group of Nobel Prize winners. Kennedy, with his quirky smile and New England charm, remarked that this was "the most extraordinary collection of talent, of human knowledge, that has ever been gathered together at the White House, with the possible exception of when Thomas Jefferson dined alone."

Every story Conger told me made its way into my spiel for the tour groups. I'm not sure the tourists ever appreciated the magnitude of where they stood, but I did.

13

Armed, Dangerous . . . and Lithe?

WHEN I WAS growing up near the Wasatch Range in Utah, little boys always had signs on the outside of their tree houses: No Girls Allowed. That's how we all felt waiting for the day the Secret Service would finally make us special agents. Every day I felt they were telling me that I didn't get to play in the tree house. It was great to have me nearby offering lemonade, but it was boys only.

After a state dinner one night, we all went out for pizza. "You guys are good and we're glad to have you. But if they make you special agents, I'll quit," one of the male agents joked.

It was ego, but my terse response was "be careful what you wish for." I knew what was coming.

Nearly a year into our tenure serving in the EPS, uniforms arrived for the five of us. We opened the boxes to find black military uniforms with heels. Phyllis scowled and said, "I'm not wearing this."

"Agents don't wear uniforms," I agreed, and I believe we made our point.

Finally, on December 15, 1971, we were instructed to report to the office of the assistant secretary of the treasury, Eugene T. Rossides, for our swearing in. He, along with Secret Service director James J. Rowley and top brass of the Secret Service, joined dignitaries and members of the press.

All five of us were collectively holding our breath. It had been a long time coming. We weren't sure they'd follow through with swearing us in. From day one, we'd fulfilled all the requirements, but there had been multiple delays or excuses.

With our backs to the cameras and flashbulbs flashing, we raised our right hands and took the oath to protect and serve our country. We were later told by one of the assistant directors that they planned to use us in counterfeit undercover work and didn't want us to be recognized—hence the anonymity during the ceremony.

So, early in December, five women were sworn in as the first female special agents in the 106-year history of the United States Secret Service, considered the most prestigious position in law enforcement and a male bastion.

In celebration, the assistant secretary of the treasury gave us each a first-strike edition of the Eisenhower silver dollar as a keepsake. Although it was a little too big to keep in my pocket for luck, I never parted with this small token that represented such a large shift in a woman's right to serve her country.

Directing our attention to James J. Rowley, an imposing man none of us had previously met, I whispered to newly appointed Special Agent Phyllis Shantz, "I think they are actually happy about this. Can you believe it?"

"Time will tell," she said. In fact, the secretary of the treasury and the director were jovial. In our first photo op, the secretary posed for a picture of Phyllis and I kissing him on each check. The men started cracking jokes themselves and everyone seemed relieved.

"We've done it now," I heard from across the room.

"Oh, what have we done?"

"Can't change it now," a deep voice chuckled from the back.

We were elated. We were special agents.

After the ceremony, we packed up our .357 Magnum revolvers and went to work. I was, finally, a bona fide United States Secret Service special agent. More women were likely carrying guns in their purses that day in the District of Columbia than anywhere else in the United States.

The next day, the *United Press International* put out an article on the wire and in several newspapers around the country with the group photo of our backs. Remarkably, the press reported on our appearances rather than our skills and accomplishments. The reporter covering our swearing-in ceremony wrote:

Women In Secret Service

WASHINGTON (UPI) (December 16, 1971)—Five young women took the oath of office today as special agents of the U. S. Secret Service and became the first of their sex to join the 106-year-old agency.

Customarily, they would be referred to as "pretty" or at least "attractive," since this is true of most young women successful in their careers. They entered the room with their faces averted, and were sworn in with their backs to photographers and television cameras.

Three are brunette, one a golden blond, and the fifth had short, frosted dark hair. All had lithe, well-shaped figures.

The women, all single, were identified as Laurie B. Anderson, 24, Jersey City, N.J., Sue A. Baker, 25, Oak Ridge, Tenn., Kathryn I. Clark, 24, Salt Lake City, Utah, Holly Hufschmidt, 28, Milwaukee, Wis., and Phyllis F. Shantz, 25, Rome, N.Y.

Miss Shantz' parents attended the brief ceremonies.

They came to the Secret Service from positions in the Executive Protective Service, a uniformed force supervised by the Secret Service. All but Miss Clark had worked formerly in the D. C. metropolitan police force. Starting salaries for the positions they now hold range from $7,000 to $9,000.

Looking back, I am amazed that we weren't offended that this reporter didn't take us more seriously. I didn't admit it at the time, but I was flattered. I know it doesn't pay homage to the historical merit of the event or what we had accomplished, but I had never been called pretty or skinny before.

I suppose I should have questioned the integrity of the article: they're describing our hair color? Seriously? Pretty or attractive? Lithe? Well-shaped figures? How about "These ladies are sharpshooters" or "They could kill you with their thumbs?" Better yet, how about "These women just swore to give their lives for their country for $8,500 a year?" But I don't think reporters, male agents, or society in general knew quite what to say. Our swearing in was groundbreaking—not earthshaking, but definitely significant, as we shot holes in the proverbial glass ceiling. Fifty years later, the picture taken of us that day hangs in the US Secret Service museum in Washington, DC.

Our higher-ups didn't provide much more of an endorsement than several national newspapers. The public affairs director stated that the service felt the "girls" would "fit in nicely." Ken Thompson, the assistant special agent in charge of the Washington Field Office, was in attendance that day and was asked by a reporter what he thought of the historic occasion. "Sure this is historic—right along with the Chicago Fire, the bombing of Pearl Harbor and the San Francisco earthquake," said Thompson.

Thompson's tongue-in-cheek comment made me laugh. Maybe this wasn't tragic, but it certainly was revolutionary. Later I realized Thompson was in a bind. Had he proclaimed it to be "history making," many of the men would have disliked him and would have dismissed the importance of our coming on board. As it was, we all walked a tightrope, so keeping a sense of humor was important. A sense of humor and a thick skin got the job done.

We were all just figuring it out, one step at a time. I suppose that's what happens when you're paving the way. Eventually, Ken Thompson became one of the biggest advocates for women in the Secret Service and another dear friend.

Executive Protective Service (EPS) Training Academy included courses in self-defense, arrest techniques, pursuit and defensive driving, riot control, and a multitude of weapons training. I was just one of the guys to my instructors.

I was the only woman in my Executive Protective Service training class, which included course work in police procedures, firearms, psychology, criminal law, first aid, laws of arrest, and search and seizure, as well as international treaties and protocols.

Everyone got a good laugh when the men voted me "Miss Congeniality" during my training class graduation.

Secret Service goes co-ed

NO FACES, PLEASE: FEMALE SECRET SERVICE AGENTS ARE SWORN IN BY EUGENE ROSSIDES.

CO-ED SECRET SERVICE—After 106 years, "Secret Servicemen" have integrated by adding five women. Eugene Rossides, assistant secretary of Treasury, administers the oath. Authorities requested that the faces remain secret.

For the first time in the 106-year history of the Secret Service, five young women took the oath of office yesterday from Eugene T. Rossides, Assistant Secretary of the Treasury Department.

Altho the still and TV cameras were out in full force, they were permitted to photograph only backs of heads and the shapely knees beneath miniskirts.

The girls just completed a year with the Executive Protection Service, the uniform branch of the Secret Service. They are Laurie B. Anderson, 24, of Jersey City, N.J., Sue A. Baker, 25, of Oak Ridge, Tenn., Kathryn I. Clark, 24, of Salt Lake City, Utah, Holly Hufschmidt, 28, of Milwaukee, Wis., and Phyllis F. Shantz, 25, of Rome, N.Y. All are university graduates.

They will be temporarily assigned to the D.C. area before entering Treasury Law Enforcement officer training school in January. After that, they will enter Secret Service Training School for special agents.

The girls were not identified. There was one startling blond, three with hair flowing over their shoulders, and one with short clipped hair. One wore suede boots and a matching suede jacket.

Rossides said, as he administered the oath, "I don't know whether you want to be called women, females, girls, or ladies, but in a few minutes I know you will want to be called secret agents."

James J. Rowley, Secret Service director, said "I'm confident these girls will do well. They have done exceptionally well during their year with E.P.S."

Their job will pay them between $7000 and $9000 a year. They are charged, as are other agents, with protection of the President and his immediate family, the Vice President, the President and Vice President elect, candidates, and will serve as sky marshalls and special customs agents.

Altho they are unmarried, being single is not a requirement for the job. Nor will pregnancy mean dismissal. They will carry weapons.

Jack Warner, director of public affairs for the agency, was asked if there had been any lip from the male agents. "None so far," he said, "but I'm sure we'll be hearing shortly."

December 15, 1971—Assistant Secretary of the Treasury Eugene T. Rossides administers the oath to the first five female US Secret Service special agents.

Swearing-In Day! (left to right): US Secret Service director James J. Rowley, Special Agents Holly Hufschmidt, Laurie B. Anderson, Phyllis F. Shantz, Kathryn Clark, Sue Ann Baker, and Assistant Secretary of the Treasury Eugene T. Rossides

Equipment issued to
me as a special agent
in 1971 included a
.357 Magnum revolver,
badge, commission
book, handcuffs, and
business cards.

KATHRYN I. CLARK
SPECIAL AGENT
U. S. SECRET SERVICE

WASHINGTON, D. C.
PHONE:

14

The Details

ONE OF THE first lessons I learned about protecting the president, the vice president, their families, and foreign heads of state was that these assignments were called "details"—the presidential detail, vice presidential detail, and so on. Agents assigned to details took on multiple tasks. During advance preparation and planning for the president—whether it was the inauguration, a visit to the site of a new homeless children's facility, or a state dinner—the Secret Service prepared for the event with the same meticulous vehemence—planning for the worst and hoping for the best. Success is in the details. It was a good lesson. More often than not, I found that to be true of life in general.

In the case of the inaugural parade, the windows in every building along Pennsylvania Avenue were secured and every manhole cover was sealed, along with a million other things. As new agents, we learned from the ground up, and we covered every base assigned in order to make the president safe and secure. We often went incognito, surveying the crowd. Frequently, we would be assigned an observation post; we stood there for hours, despite heat, rain, or snow.

During the inaugural parade, the president and first lady generally ride in an armor-plated limousine—called the "Beast" today—and the Secret Service does what it was trained to do—follow a complex plan called the advance. When the president and first lady decide to leave the limousine and work the crowd, shaking hands and hugging babies, their protection becomes far more challenging. Agents surround them, doing their best to ward off tragedy in an unsecured crowd. The president can do whatever he wants and has the option to leave his vehicle and greet the line of admirers; the agents do not have a choice. The Secret Service is trained to respond to the president's decisions. When protecting the president in this circumstance, you are said to be "working the line," and it is one of the most important and difficult tasks of a special agent.

Much of the time, Secret Service agents stand in the shadow of the person they are protecting. They wear dark glasses, an earpiece, and a radio with a tiny microphone that dangles down the sleeve of their dark suits. They are in constant communication with the command post, and the bulge of a weapon is prominent on their hips. They look tough, and they like it that way. The dark glasses disguise their eyes as they scan the crowds. The public doesn't know where they are looking as they look at everyone and everything. That persona is just part of the many elements that make up the detail.

While I worked a number of presidential details, I was never assigned to one permanently. No woman was. A few years after I left the service, however, women were assigned permanently to presidential and vice presidential details, including Mary Ann Gordon to the presidential detail in July 1978 and Phyllis Shantz to the vice presidential detail in August 1978.

Training for the variety of assignments in the worlds of protection and criminal investigation never stopped. Ongoing classes were taught by senior agents. We were drilled in the use of all types of weapons, hand-to-hand combat, criminal investigation, counterfeit detection, and planning for protection of the president and his family no matter where they were or where they were going.

We were trained to expect anything and everything in an attack or a kidnapping attempt—snipers on a roof, a sideswipe with multiple assailants and high-powered weapons coming at us, along with a host of other possibilities. You name it, we were trained to anticipate and handle it.

It became clear, however, that nothing could truly prepare us for what we would face. We simply had to assess the situation and be good enough to make the right call at the right time. "Play it by ear" and "trust your gut" were the answers most often given in response to our wide-eyed questions, which usually began with "What if . . ."

One of the most powerful stories I remember during training—

whether it is true or apocryphal—was told by an instructor who had served on multiple details protecting family members of the president. The point of the story was to drive home the fact that we would have to make split-second decisions that weren't outlined in the training manual for a protective detail and often involved several high-maintenance individuals and scenarios you simply couldn't plan for. To say you had to "play it by ear" was an understatement. The story involved a time when he had to make one of those precarious, on-the-spot decisions.

On this particular rainy day, the instructor had been assigned to protect the president's daughter, who was attending a special event at the construction site of a new federal building with her father. She and members of her detail arrived just before the official motorcade. The advance agent had planned for everything but the weather. Sheets of rain were pummeling the arrival site. Large crowds had gathered for an opportunity to see the president and his family. Umbrellas of every shape and color cloaked the mass of onlookers, making it difficult to scan the noisy crowds. Undaunted by the rain, they were cheering and waving flags and signs.

The first daughter was dressed in a stunning white dress and white linen shoes, and she was not pleased with her agent, who was leading her across a muddy parking lot. He was on double duty, scanning the crowds while maneuvering his protectee to a dry spot near the podium.

At that point, the agent telling the story said he had just gotten radio notification in his earpiece that the president's limousine was two minutes from arrival.

As they moved toward the stage, the agents did their job to protect the first daughter—looking for anything out of the ordinary. And there it was—the muzzle of what appeared to be a rifle with a scope protruding out of the crowd.

The agent alerted the other agents, screaming into his microphone, "Gun! Gun! Gun!"

Our instructor said he pulled his gun and pushed her to the ground, covering her body with his own, shielding her while he aimed his weapon at the crowd and screamed, "Get down! Get down! Get back!"

While relaying the story, the agent talked grimly about his split-second hesitation when he decided not to pull the trigger. If he had made the wrong call, he and the young woman he was protecting could have been killed along with other agents and civilians in the crowd. If he had made the wrong call, and the gun in the crowd was aimed at the arriving president of the United States, history as we know it would have taken a dramatic turn.

"Something wasn't right," he said. "One detail was wrong. The gun was too low—too low to be shouldered by an adult and too high to be resting on a chair."

In a split second, he had to decide—shoot or don't shoot. He held the shot. When the confusion and fear settled, an eight-year-old boy walked out of the crowd with his father's deer rifle. He had wanted to see the president and thought he could get a better view through the scope on the gun.

The agent obviously made the right call.

Agents hustled the boy away while the lead agent apologized and helped the young woman up from the muddy pavement. Her dress was ruined and her knees were bloodied. She was grateful, but she wasn't happy.

The agent said he was reassigned to the midnight shift on former first lady Mamie Eisenhower's detail in the dead of winter. I don't believe any of this was true, but the morale of the story was not lost on me or my fellow agents as an example of what could happen on any given day.

15

WFO: New Day, New Assignment

IN EARLY 1971, the Secret Service assigned 1,145 male special agents to field offices in major cities around the country. In December 1971, five women were added. Unlike the male agents before us, we women arrived by a rather circuitous path. Now that we were special agents, the five of us were reassigned to the Washington Field Office (WFO). We had proven to be valuable on details with temporary protectees, such as candidates and foreign dignitaries, and now it was time for more permanent duty.

The United States Secret Service is world renowned for the physical protection it provides to the nation's highest elected leaders and other government officials. However, the Secret Service was created in 1865 to investigate and prevent counterfeiting and check fraud. Despite the enormity of the dual responsibility, the Secret Service claims it makes for better agents in both roles and has remained stalwart in that belief to this day.

While the protection mission is known worldwide, the Secret Service's investigative mission continues to grow because of developments in technology. Special agents investigate credit card, internet, and cloud-based fraud as well as computer-based attacks on the nation's banking and telecommunications. In the 1970s, computers were just being developed and most agents had never seen one. Our counterfeiters weren't technologically driven, but there were plenty of other ways to commit fraud. They made bogus money the old-fashioned way—they printed it.

Our criminal investigations of financial crimes were focused primarily on catching counterfeiters any way we could. Not long after I landed at the WFO, I got my chance to hit the streets working undercover alongside male agents buying counterfeit money and making arrests. It was a long way from giving tours at the White House as an EPS officer.

I reported for duty at the WFO, an ordinary-looking office building a few blocks from the White House. This time I drove to work in my official vehicle, a dull gray Rambler sedan with a little wire antenna on the top and a red magnetic light under the front seat. It was attached to a long wire, so I could slam it on the roof in an emergency. Although my space in the parking garage was the farthest from the elevator, at least I didn't have to take the bus.

Exiting the elevator, I encountered a weary agent sitting at a plain wooden desk with a Secret Service seal hanging on the wall. With little fanfare, he asked for my identification. Being the designated paper-checking greeter at the field office was as boring as standing post in the middle of the night. I presented my credentials—my new black commission book with a star-shaped Secret Service badge embedded on the leather cover. There was no big grin and no "Hi, Kathryn! Welcome to WFO!" Instead, he flipped it open and scanned my name and picture. I wasn't sure he was going to believe me. After all, I didn't really believe it myself. Right under Kathryn Clark, it said US Secret Service Agent.

The agent's general lack of enthusiasm and shrugged shoulders made him appear older and more fatigued. He stared at me a few seconds longer than was comfortable for either of us. As was often the case, he had not expected a female agent. Female agents were rumored to exist, but I'm not sure many field agents believed we were real. Everywhere I went this gray fog followed me. I was real. A bona fide female Secret Service special agent, but I wasn't a desired commodity; rather I was regarded with hesitancy. That didn't change anything for me; I was in it for the long haul, and although the whole concept of a woman entering his workplace seemed to wear him out even more, the agent passed me through.

The office was filled with fit, good-looking men sitting at government-issue desks piled with files and paperwork that appeared to spill out of the old cabinets that lined the walls. Most wore white shirts and had .357 Magnum revolvers in their shoulder holsters or jammed in the waistband of their pants. Their suit coats, with Secret Service ID pins on the left lapel, hung on the backs of oak chairs on casters. The place was loud. Some had their feet on their desk as they hollered to other agents across the room about a case or a court appearance. Then there were the undercover guys—scruffy, with dark, flashing eyes, deep into the role they were playing that day.

I stood out with my heavy leather purse slung clumsily over my left shoulder. Special Agent in Charge (SAIC) Charlie Gittens, the first African American agent in the service, leaned out of his glass office door and yelled, "Hey Clark, come into my office."

With that, I figured I was supposed to be there.

The Washington Field Office afforded me the opportunity to investigate criminal cases, and some very interesting ones at that. Working with the men in the field, I quickly learned that I didn't have to be just good if I were going to succeed, I had to be great. When you are the exception, not the rule, you must go above and beyond. Even if it is subconscious, people are waiting for you to fail. There's an added pressure there. I needed to be a good agent for myself, and more importantly, so that other women would one day have the opportunity to be agents. That kind of pressure would scare anyone. It was crucial to keep a dose of levity in my pocket as well. Instead, I focused on excelling at my job, which was exhilarating and quite fun.

One day, an experienced senior agent, Charlie Miller, drew the black bean or short straw—me as a partner. We were sent to a neighborhood in a rough part of Southeast Washington to investigate a case where an elderly woman, Mary Mitchel, had been cashing federal checks made out to someone else. As we walked down the long hallway of the low-income housing project, we could hear music playing from the apartment long before we got there. It was the first time Charlie had been assigned a female partner. He wasn't particularly comfortable with it, and he had a slight chip on his shoulder. There was some resentment, and I hadn't even done anything yet. We found the apartment and took our positions on either side of the heavy metal door. The *Shaft* theme song was blaring, and a strange shuffling sound was coming from under the door. One of the rules in making an arrest is to do it quickly. If you wait too long, evidence goes down the toilet or out the window, and suspects escape out the back door.

"Secret Service!" he shouted, banging on the door.

Nothing happened. He banged again. Again nothing. He looked at me with a crooked smile. At this point, we had pulled our weapons from their holsters.

"If you are so tough, you break down the door!" he mumbled.

Keep in mind, this man weighed more than two hundred pounds and looked like a linebacker for the Dallas Cowboys.

I smirked at him and said, "You break down the door, and I'll shoot 'em. I'm a better shot than you are!"

It definitely broke the tension. He even cracked a small smile. Fortunately, neither of us had to break down the door because at that moment, eighty-five-year-old Mary opened the door, shuffling in her pink house shoes, and hollered, "What, what . . . what you want? I'm deaf as a post!"

Mary quickly turned down the radio and immediately agreed to quit cashing the checks that had been delivered to her mailbox by mistake every month. Seems she thought it was a "present" from Uncle Sam.

Had I tried to break down the door to prove a point, I would have made a fool of myself and left with a broken shoulder. More importantly, I have always been glad I didn't shoot her. Eventually, Agent Miller and I became great friends and good partners.

Every day at the WFO came with a different assignment, a different challenge. Some days I was put on temporary assignments with the Protective Intelligence Division.

More protection is accomplished in the Secret Service field offices than people think. Protection goes well beyond surrounding the individual with well-armed agents, because part of the mission of the Secret Service is preventing an incident before it occurs. The agency relies on meticulous advance work and threat assessments developed by its Intelligence Division to identify potential risks to protectees.

Determining whether an individual is "of protective interest at the time" was one of the most challenging calls I had to make as a special agent. We were regularly sent to interview individuals who had made threats against the president. Often they were people with mental disorders and delusions.

Agents must investigate the many threats made against our nation's leaders. Often people say they weren't serious, that they were just kidding. What they don't understand is that threatening the president of the United States is a class E felony. It consists of knowingly or willfully mailing or otherwise making any threat to take the life of, kidnap, or inflict bodily harm upon the president of the United States. This also includes presidential candidates and former presidents.

Ferreting out threats against the president may not have been as sophisticated in my day as it is now with certain technological advances, but eliminating the threats was no less important. With the stakes about as high as they come, defending the leader of the free world, you had to keep your wits about you and your sense of humor intact.

One steamy summer day in Washington, I was assigned to a protective intelligence response team at the Headquarters Building near the White House. Sitting with his tie loosened around his neck and a pencil behind his ear, an agent answered a special phone line where questionable calls are forwarded by White House operators. I was surprised to find that then—and now—the White House phone number is listed in the phone book. I can assure you the president doesn't answer, but if you are making threats, this agent does.

On that day, a man calling himself "The Electric Man" said his body was charged with electricity and it was the president's fault. Screaming into the phone, he told the agent he was calling from a phone booth a block from the White House and he was on his way to get the president.

Another agent and I were dispatched to investigate. Arriving at the designated phone booth, we saw a small crowd of gawkers gathering around our suspect, whose agitation was escalating. My partner and I approached him and identified ourselves as Secret Service agents. I decided to play the "good cop," suggesting in a kindly manner that he should come with us and we would help him sort out his problem.

I reached toward his upper arm to guide him out of the booth, but just before my hand touched his arm he yelled, "Don't touch me! If you touch me, the electricity in my body will kill you!"

I retreated, then moved toward him again. "Don't touch me!" he screamed.

Waving his arms, he dropped the phone. Swinging wildly on the aluminum cord, the black handset smashed into the glass and metal walls of the booth. The crowd began to yell.

"Leave him alone, you pigs!" they jeered. "Pigs" was the endearing term and favorite street name for law enforcement officers, adopted and propagated by the antiwar movement, the counterculture of the 1960s and 1970s.

I cautiously stepped back and nodded at my partner, who pulled his handcuffs out of his belt and moved forward to slap one around Mr. Electric's wrist. With that, the crowd moved closer to witness the outcome. Everyone was a bit on edge, although we felt certain he did not have a weapon. "Easy does it," I said, speaking to him as you would to a spooked horse. "It's okay. We're not going to hurt you."

"Zzzzz zzzzzz," he yelled as I again extended my hand to him.

"No one is going to kill you. Not with electricity, not with anything. I don't want you to hurt me or any of these people. We don't want to hurt you; you don't want to hurt us."

Every time I would move in, he'd convulse and shriek, "Zzzzz."

Dealing with psychotic people was part of the job; the mentally ill often focused their fears and threats on people in power, and it doesn't get much more powerful than the president of the United States. "Come with me and we'll sort it out," I said as I tried to calmly beckon him in my direction.

He was silent for a moment as we all held our breath. Then, just as my partner's handcuff touched the man's wrist, the crazed, wide-eyed Electric Man let out a sound of electricity that mimicked who knows how many volts. "Zzzzzzz zzzzzzzzzzzzz zzzzzzzz!"

Everyone gave a collective gasp. The crowd roared as my fellow agent dropped the cuffs on the metal floor. Embarrassed and angry at this point, he composed himself enough to pick up the cuffs and slap them on Electric Man's wrists. Placing him under arrest, we pushed him in the car and hustled him off to St. Elizabeth's Psychiatric Hospital.

On the way back to headquarters, we agreed to never reveal we were almost taken down by a telephone. Walking into the squad room, we were told by one of the agents with a Cheshire cat grin, "The special agent in charge wants to see you."

"Not a word," said my partner with a slant of his eyes. I nodded.

"Well," the SAIC said with a chortle. "How did your investigation go?"

"Fine," I mumbled. "Not a serious threat. We transported him to St. Elizabeth's."

Putting on a serious face he said, "You forgot to do one thing."

"Sir?" my partner responded.

"You forgot to hang up the damn phone!" he exclaimed.

At that, the entire office roared. Rarely did anything stay secret. The call had been put through to his office and had been placed on a speaker.

Every Electric Man threat, epitaph, gasp, and "Zzzzzzzz," followed by the sound of the cuffs hitting the floor and the jeers of the crowd, had been reported blow by blow on the phone that was still swinging on its cord in the phone booth on Fourteenth Street and Pennsylvania Avenue.

Just another day at the Washington Field Office.

16

Playing the Part

"HEY, CLARK," SAIC Charlie Gittens yelled at me though the open door of his office. I'm fairly certain no one knew my first name. They only called me Clark; maybe it was gender neutral; maybe it was easier for them to bark; maybe they couldn't decide between Kathryn or Kathy, so Clark it was.

"Headquarters has decided to try you in New York on a counterfeit gig. You'll probably be there four weeks. Give your cases to somebody else. You leave tomorrow," he informed me with his hands crossed on the top of his bald head and his feet crossed on the desk.

Here we go again, I thought. They are going to "try me." He must have sensed my concern.

"Oh, you'll do all right," he said. "Just don't let them know you're scared. Old man Whitaker can smell fear."

I didn't have any background in police work and had never worked undercover, yet they picked me to be the only female agent attached to a special anticounterfeiting task force with six men. It seems that the passing of bogus one-hundred-dollar bills on the streets of New York City was at an all-time high, and we were supposed to help squelch it.

I flew into LaGuardia and was met by another agent assigned to the task force. He was a short African American man wearing a floor-length black coat and small, round silver glasses, with a silver pick stuck in his

Afro. He introduced himself as Bill. Bill had grown up in DC and had given up his plans for the Catholic priesthood to join the Secret Service. I guess we all got there somehow.

Wearing my White House tour guide basic blue dress and navy heels, I stuck out like a sore thumb. Bill smiled and said, "I hope you brought some different clothes."

When our crew first arrived at the New York Field Office (NYFO), everyone was surprised to see a woman in the group. I was surprised to see a guy handcuffed to his chair in the middle of the squad room. Seems this agent had been caught keeping some counterfeit money from a buy for his own use. Al Whitaker, the crusty SAIC, told them to let him sit there all day while his fellow agents worked around him before they arrested him and took him to jail. His point was well taken. I had heard old man Whitaker was tough and didn't take any guff from anyone, especially his agents.

On the first day, we reported to Whitaker's office. He saw me and closed the door. I stood awkwardly in the middle of the room, as I unintentionally eavesdropped on his blustery conversation with the assistant special agent in charge about "who the hell the girl in the silly blue dress was." With great force, the door opened.

"Okay, paaark yourself and get to work!" he bellowed.

He pointed to a spot near the corner. "That's your desk." Agent Whitaker scared me, but I straightened my "silly" dress, stood a little taller, and crossed the room to my desk. I was selected for this assignment for good reason, and I wasn't going to let an intimidating, crotchety man who was supposedly on my team deter me.

The NYFO wasn't much different from the WFO aside from the aesthetics. This office could have been a gangster movie set in the 1950s. Everything was a worn army green. I could just barely see the New York skyline through filthy windowpanes. Most of the fluorescent bulbs were missing, casting a dull yellow haze like the stain on one's fingers from smoking a cigarette without a filter. Pigeons on the windowsills flapped and flew away when I walked by to my desk.

Stacks of files in sliding piles of disarray appeared to be unopened. Many of the chairs were empty. These desks held too many cases and not enough agents. Investigations were made on the street, and everyone hated paperwork anyway.

The phones rang constantly. They were the old black kind with a tangled curly cord, six plastic buttons along the front for each line, and a red one for "Hold." They all seemed to flash at once.

"Hey, Claaark," someone hollered, "call for you on line two. Agent Angelone."

This was the first of many times I would work with Special Agent Angie Angelone. While he had come to the service with a master's degree, a stint in the Marine Corps, and a career as a wrestling coach in Rockaway Beach, New York, no one would have suspected his background. On most days, his olive-toned Italian skin sported a three-day growth of well-trimmed beard accented by a cigar clenched between his teeth. His thinning black hair was slicked back and caught in a tight ponytail. Wearing a shiny gray Qiana suit and platform shoes, Angie definitely looked the part of a New York City criminal. He appeared every bit the mob boss with the pointed collar of his fitted white shirt and his gray silk tie slung loosely around his neck.

"I need a girlfriend to take along tonight," Angie said. "Are you game?"

"Sure," I said. "Give me an hour."

"Oh, and you gotta look sexy," he chuckled. "Have you ever worked a hooker beat?"

For a Colorado sorority girl "just off the bus" in New York City, this was going to be a challenge, but I wasn't going to let him know that. "I haven't. It won't be an issue. I'm your girl."

"Tonight you will be," Angie guffawed as he ended the call.

I was glad I had noticed a thrift shop near the office. There I found the perfect pieces for my costume—a pair of tight, shiny black pants, sky-high heels, and a bright red low-cut rayon blouse. I had my eyes on a silk blouse, but I couldn't afford it.

In the restroom, I teased out my shoulder-length hair, rimmed my eyes with black eyeliner, and poured on "Love That Red" lipstick. I looked in the mirror. I think I looked like a hooker, but I had never met one.

Special Agent Whitaker softened a bit when I arrived later that afternoon for the hooker assignment. The squad room erupted in cat calls and laughter as I struck a pose in my high heels with very pointed toes.

"Hi, Angie," I said. "Sexy enough for you?" He didn't feel the need to respond, but he walked back into his office with a smile on his face.

After seeing my transformation, the men seemed willing for me to participate. I guess they figured I might give them an edge in their undercover operations. From then on out, I would play the girlfriend of seasoned undercover agents who were working the street. They could take me along on a "buy" without creating suspicion.

When you make a buy, you have to have two or more agents in on the deal. One actually makes the buy while the other is there to back up his partner and testify in court. Introducing another agent was often one of the most difficult parts of the deal.

Counterfeiters had to sell their goods, but they were always on the lookout for the Secret Service. It takes many meetings for an agent like Angie Angelone to earn their trust and make a buy. That's how you catch them. When an undercover agent makes a buy with good money and the exchange takes place, then you've got an arrest.

When Angie and I were alone, I got the reaction I wanted. "Hey, baby," he said. "Now that's what I mean. One question, where's your piece?"

"Right here," I said, flipping open my sparkly handbag.

"We will just have to make sure they don't search you," he said, flipping a piece of Dubble Bubble gum my way. "Smack that and get an attitude. Just tell them that nobody touches you but me. I think they will back off. These punks have never seen a hooker working for the service. You'll do just fine. Just remember you're my cover. They'll frisk me so I can't carry. If things go bad, you're all we've got."

"Got it," I said, popping a big pink bubble with my red lips.

I have to admit, I kinda liked it. I think I always wanted to be an actress. This just happened to be a role with a twist. In this casting, I might have to shoot somebody. The bullets were real, and when the action started, I had to do anything necessary to protect Angie.

Angie motioned to me with a nod, and we joined six other agents in the squad room. It was the first time I'd been invited to a briefing. No longer in suits and ties, the men were dressed to blend into the neighborhood landscape and make arrests. The squad room was in the same disarray as the rest of the field office. Abused metal ashtrays filled with cigarette butts and a few cigars sat in the middle of a long wooden table. White foam cups with remnants of that morning's coffee sat, long forgotten. Not one cup had a lipstick print.

Eyeing the cigar butts, one of the guys winked at me and whispered, "Angie always hands out cigars if we make the buy."

In his New York street slang, Angie explained the plan. "Clark and I will pick up the two perps in the Volkswagen. Guys in the motor pool fixed it so that once they get in the back seat, they won't be gettin' out."

One guy was skeptical and called out, "What's Clark's cover?"

"These bums aren't going to think anything of it," Angie retorted. "I couldn't believe they brought dames into the service. Neither will they."

"They might not believe a hooker this good-looking is with you," one of the guys chortled.

"Enough," Angie growled, but he was smiling.

Already in character, his New York accent rolling off his tongue, Angie told us the good money would be stowed in the front trunk of the VW.

"She'll drive. Her piece is in her purse under the front seat," he said. I patted my little bag and smiled.

"I'll tell 'em they have to get in the back for cover. Once I check the meat, I'll give you the signal. I'll open the trunk lid and light my cigar," he said, waving his well-chewed stogie in the air. "Yous guys got it? Nobody moves until I blow the smoke."

I don't know why, but he always alluded to counterfeit bills as "meat." We picked up the two counterfeiters on the prearranged street corner in a dicey neighborhood in Brooklyn called Bedford-Stuyvesant. The perps were "cool," with their black platform shoes and more gold chains around their necks than most Texas women I know. Thank goodness we had dressed the part. Jammed in the waistbands of their bell-bottomed pants, each man had a semiautomatic pistol. At the time, they were the biggest guns I had ever seen.

At first they didn't like the car or me. "Screw it then," Angie shouted, and he got back in the car. "Drive. And step on it!"

I jammed the stick shift into first and hit the gas. It wasn't fifty feet before they raced after us. "Okay," Angie said. "Let 'em in."

They pushed their way into the back seat. "Do you have the meat?" Angie said, nodding toward a briefcase one had across his lap.

"Yeah," one of the guys said.

The other muttered under his breath, "I don't like the bitch."

"Watch your mouth," Angie growled. "She's my girl. Let's have a little respect or you can pedal your shit somewhere else."

We parked the car on a dimly lit side street where an older woman was sweeping her front porch. Not a good spot, I thought, but there wasn't time to warn her.

Angie checked the case, thumbing through stacks of reasonable facsimiles of one-hundred-dollar bills.

"Okay," he said, "I've got the money up front."

He got out, slammed the door, and lit the cigar. All hell broke loose! Red lights, sirens, and Secret Service agents appeared out of nowhere, leaving me with two very agitated thugs pinned in the back seat of the car struggling to get to their guns. I grabbed my purse, opened the door, and rolled under the car, kicking the door shut with my left foot.

The agents grabbed the two men and Angie, making an equal-opportunity arrest so we wouldn't blow his cover. Under the car, I kicked at a beefy agent whose hand was around my ankle, and I screamed words I didn't know I knew as loudly as I could. I had to play the part and they had to arrest me, or my cover would be blown as well.

During all the mayhem, the old lady who had been watching the whole thing go down started hitting the arresting agent with her broom.

"You leave that little white girl alone, you honky pig," she yelled. "She didn't do nothin'."

I thanked her as they cuffed me and pushed me into the back seat of the Secret Service sedan. I've never done drugs, but I'm not sure there is anything that gives you the same high as a night working undercover.

In a few blocks they uncuffed me, and we drove back to the field office. As promised, Angie handed out the cigars. The first one was to me. I didn't smoke, but I took a triumphant puff. It tasted surprisingly good, but maybe that was the victory I was tasting.

Angie and I made a great team. He trusted me and was willing to teach me. As an experienced undercover agent, he genuinely liked having a female partner. I hadn't expected such a warm welcome, but I think that our partnership is what the Secret Service was looking for when they brought women into the fold. For Angie, my being a woman was an asset, a difference to be celebrated and utilized in the best ways possible.

17

Cheeseburgers and Counterfeiters

ONE FALL afternoon, an agent sat on a stool behind a peephole inside Dandy Dan's ice cream truck, which was parked on a street in Queens. Three other agents and I sat in a dirty brown Ford Fairlane sedan watching for any movement of our suspect. We had been watching for hours. That's what you do on surveillance—you watch and wait, you wait and watch.

Normally we would have stormed in and arrested the perp, but this counterfeiter/armed robber was bad news, so it was important that we arrested him outside rather than in his workplace. He wasn't a cop killer, but he had a bad reputation among law enforcement. I wasn't sure what earned him this label, but he was an unscrupulous dude and we weren't taking any risks.

I wasn't entirely sure what his business was; the building we were outside wasn't fancy. It was a rummy little joint, a front for something sketchy, that's for sure.

We were tired and hungry. I had a pretty gray suede blazer draped across my lap. It was getting hot, but it hid my gun, so I kept the leather tucked firmly around my body.

The lead agent picked up the microphone and radioed Dandy Dan. "Hey Dan. Any action on your end?"

"Nope," he said.

"We're going to send Clark into this burger joint to grab some lunch. Any problem with that?" he questioned.

"Nah. I don't know if the creep will ever come out," the ice cream truck replied.

I was the rookie agent. It was my job to get lunch. Each agent took five dollars from his wallet, and I exited the vehicle.

"Four burgers and four regular coffees," I ordered through an outside window.

The guy in the window wore a white paper hat and a dirty apron. Probably great burgers, I thought as I paid him. He handed me the change, four large cups of coffee, and a bag with grease already seeping through the paper. Gingerly, I threaded the bills through my fingers, held the coins in my palm, and balanced two cups of coffee in each hand. I was the rookie. I wasn't going to screw up. My first time grabbing the coffees, I'd made the mistake of ordering black coffees and the guys hadn't let it go for weeks. How was the DC girl, originally from Colorado, supposed to know that a "regular coffee" in New York meant one cream and one sugar?

Walking toward the car I heard Dan yell over the radio, "He's on the move. Go! Go! Go! He's getting in the black sedan. Move! Move or you'll lose him!"

My shift leader had already started the car. "Get in, Clark. Get in, Clark," they yelled, and there I stood, the rookie lunch lady with teetering coffee cups in both hands. Luckily, there was a large trash can within arm's reach; I dumped everything, the change included, and jumped into the car. I was halfway in the car as they peeled out. My foot scraped on the side of the road, and just as I slammed the door shut, we passed him. He turned and we were still going straight. Tearing down the street after what we thought was the black car, we heard Dan from his ice cream surveillance truck scream, "You're going the wrong way! Turn around!"

Without skipping a beat, we gunned across the curb of the center island, the big engine racing as the belly of the Fairlane scraped over cement, grass, and several small bushes. There was a loud thump when the wheels came off the island onto the road, and our car pulled in behind the correct black car. Our driver slapped a magnetic cherry-red light on the roof and flipped on the siren. We were no longer undercover; we were in a high-speed chase.

The speedometer hit ninety-four miles per hour as we flew over a railroad crossing. Another car joined us, cutting off the perp. Cornered, he finally stopped. The guys leaped out of the car, guns drawn. When they pulled him out of his car and draped him over the trunk, I got a good look at him. He was overweight and disheveled, bearded, with wild hair and a really bad attitude. When they unbuckled his pants to check for weapons, they fell to his ankles.

The guys frisked and cuffed him. I pointed my service revolver at him, providing backup for the other agents as they holstered their guns and prepared to walk the suspect to the car.

"Get that broad out of here. What's she doing here?" he yelled, eyeing my large weapon, which I was still pointing at him.

It was the first time I'd ever drawn down on someone, which means I had the gun pointed directly at his head. I'd always wondered what that would actually be like.

"Get the bitch out of here, she's going to kill me," he ranted.

"Federal agent, don't move. Secret Service. You're under arrest," I declared boldly.

"How could you give a broad a gun? Are you crazy?" He stared at me wild eyed.

All the guys had holstered their weapons by this point. The lead agent laughed. Looking directly at the suspect, he said, "Go ahead and shoot him, Clark."

At that point his pants were not only below his knees, they were wet.

18

Girl Undercover

"TWO HUNDRED sixty thousand, two hundred seventy thousand, two hundred eighty thousand. It's all here," I thought to myself, as I wiped my perspiring palms against my slacks. "Yeah, twenty-eight hundred one-hundred-dollar bills. Two hundred eighty thousand dollars. I've never seen that much money except on television," I thought, slamming the briefcase shut and closing the clasp.

It was the morning of a buy, and my first assignment was to walk a few blocks down the street to pick up $280,000 from the Federal Reserve Bank. I was to count the money and sign for it, then walk it back to the office in a simple briefcase. Easy as that, right? Make sure you don't miscount funds totaling many times more than your annual earnings. If I miscounted, I would be hard pressed to pay it back on my meager salary.

"Isn't anyone going with me?" I had asked. "Oh, there will be a couple of guys behind you," Agent Angelone had mumbled. "But this way, we won't attract any attention. Nobody would think a little gal like you would have that much money in her purse."

So I picked up the money, and this "little gal" walked down the streets of New York with a briefcase full of expensive bait.

It was chilly and gray outside, and a patchy drizzle covered the streets. Grabbing my trench coat that morning had been a wise choice. Seemed like early mornings in the bowels of New York were always drab—like a city with a hangover. It took some time to wake up. When I met the guys out front, they pulled up in a beat-up gray sedan from the Secret Service motor pool, a confiscated vehicle from an earlier counterfeit bust that smelled and ran badly.

"Happy belated birthday, Kathy. You have fun last night?" asked Agent Miller, the New York City local who sat at the desk adjacent to mine.

"It was no Clyde's, but it did just fine."

"Oh yeah, who is Clyde?" he chuckled.

Clyde's, on M Street, was my favorite restaurant in DC. It was where my friends would have taken me to celebrate my birthday had I not been working undercover in New York. Instead I spent the evening of October 11 with a motley bunch from the NYFO who carried guns better than a tune. Five scruffy guys sitting around two rumpled beds at Manhattan's not-so-famous Downtowner Motel had crooned my birthday wishes over a lackluster candle lifted from the bar downstairs, and we'd washed down a tiny cake from the deli next door with bottles of warm beer. That's about the best you could do with a twenty-five-dollar per diem. And it suited me well enough.

"Thanks. It was nice to have the night off," I responded, ignoring Miller's jokes. Men will always be men.

"That is rare, indeed," he stated.

And with that we were walking into the NYFO squad room, where Angie was already barking orders to the detail. Personal lives weren't of much consequence when you were in the Secret Service. The counterfeit task force from DC had done its best and I was grateful, but it was time to focus.

Angie had been working a big case involving hundreds of thousands of dollars and the buy was set to go down at JFK Airport. In theory, a buy is simple: a pair of undercover agents brings real money to buy the counterfeit bills. The first agent initiates the actual exchange of goods. A second agent is present for the first agent's protection and to corroborate the details of the arrest in court.

But, as is usually the case, nothing is as simple as it seems on paper. The bad guys, a.k.a. the alleged counterfeiters, were spooked when Angie wanted to bring another guy along. Enter me. I had the perfect cover—I was female. No one would ever suspect me of being an agent. Same as on the hooker beat.

Strangely, there were no classes in Treasury Law Enforcement School that taught "Undercover 101: Acting the Part." The point of a "cover" is to hide your identity as a federal agent. No matter the assignment, an agent's anonymity is as important as a weapon in making an arrest or providing another circle of protection.

Slipping into and out of my "cover" both in protection and in counterfeit investigations came easily for me. I found the characters I was asked to play exciting and a little scary. Whether I was a street hooker, a pistol-packing nanny, a guest at a state dinner, or a stewardess calling the shots, I played lots of roles and I liked it.

That night I would be the eyes and ears of a half-million-dollar counterfeit buy and arrest. I would be there to protect Angie if things went south. He was not going to be carrying a weapon. I was.

Suited up like I was off to Europe on Pan Am, I looked like a stewardess, with an ID badge, flight bag, and trench coat—the standard issue, with the exception of my .357 Magnum revolver in a shoulder holster. I'd consider that quite the upgrade to a traditional flight attendant's attire. Sitting a few footsteps away from the locker where Angie would store the money, I was wired with a radio jammed in the belt of my slacks and a microphone embedded in a Chapstick tube dangling down the sleeve of my coat. With an earpiece in my left ear, I was in business.

Other agents were dressed as ticket agents, baggage handlers, and tourists. Angie looked like an Italian mafioso, wearing the same shiny gray suit he'd had on when I met him, a starched white shirt with the collar popped up in the back, and a silk tie flipped over rather than tied. He had a two-day growth of neatly trimmed beard.

I looked the part. He looked the part. We all did. That was the fun part of working undercover.

We didn't know how they were going to deliver half a million in hundred-dollar bills to the middle of the airport. They just told Angie to bring the money and come alone; they would take care of the rest. Most of these deals went down in public places. I am not sure why, but they did.

Everyone was in position. The command post did a radio check. Everyone acknowledged.

"Clark," the agent in charge said. "You know the drill—it's on your call. Communicate with Angie once he hooks up. It's a go when he lights his cigar!"

"Roger," I snapped while applying my Chapstick.

Here we go—but it didn't go. Angie wandered aimlessly near the locker where we had stowed the briefcase. No one appeared.

"Clark, report!" crackled the command post.

"Nothing," I replied. "No sign of the meat." I still had no idea why Angie called the counterfeit money "meat," but I accepted it as part of his persona.

Finally, after giving me and the surrounding area a close look, one of the felons walked up to Angie. I suspected he was suspicious of me, so I pulled out a flight schedule book and did my best to look like I was who I was supposed to be. I guess it worked because he stood close to Angie, mouthing words I couldn't hear.

"The perp is here, but no audio," I whispered.

The guy left, and Angie came over and sat next to me. Suddenly, he started snapping his fingers and humming like he was killing time, looking cool. I listened closely. What he was singing wasn't on the top of the billboard charts, for sure!

"There are two in a car . . . parked at the taxi stand," he sang, snapping in rhythm.

"One has a heater . . . delayed in delivery . . . meat coming in a locker. Stay cool . . . fifteen minutes till smoke gets in your eye," Angie mused.

We never made eye contact, but I had all I needed to report. In fifteen minutes, the deal went down.

Here they came, wheeling a large brown military trunk through the lobby. Angie looked in the trunk, lit his cigar, and started to open the locker.

"Go, go, go!" I said into my Chapstick. "The cigar is lit!"

Agents appeared from everywhere, arresting all the crooks and Angie. He was taken to jail with the rest of them to preserve his cover.

Later that night, we went to the "Tombs" to spring Angie. I liked him a lot and was concerned about him having to spend the night in jail. I had heard that this particular facility was a terrible place, and they made prisoners give up their shoes to check for contraband or razor blades. When we picked Angie up, his shoes were intact.

"You're looking no worse for the wear. How'd you keep your cover and your shoes?"

"I told 'em 'I ain't got no toes' and they left me alone," he chuckled. "You always have to have a story, kiddo. Keeps you out of trouble. If you don't have one, make it up as you go."

Working undercover in New York City during a counterfeit buy at JFK Airport.

A counterfeit bust in New York City (me in the ponytail)

Another special agent joins me at the New York Field Office to celebrate a trunk load of bogus bills after the successful buy.

When you're an undercover agent in 1972, it's important to keep a receipt when "borrowing" $280,000 cash from the Federal Reserve Bank to be used when making a counterfeit buy!

Me celebrating with Special Agent Angie Angelone's promised cigar after a successful counterfeit bust.

19

Make Love, Not War

WHEN I returned to Washington in the spring of 1972, the city's landscape was changing. Marches were growing into violent protests fueled by hate, discontent, anger, racial tension, civil disobedience, and disruption. The Vietnam War was escalating and the compulsory military service, otherwise known as the draft, was requiring more men to fight. Some were responding "Hell no! We won't go!" while others who had served honorably were coming home to disrespect, spit in the face, and being called names like "Baby Killers!" The antiwar movement was beginning to feel more like a revolution, even the beginning of a civil war. On the streets, law enforcement was the enemy; they'd been reduced to a four-letter word: "Pigs!"

The government was the adversary—particularly the president of the United States. Multiple assassination threats against President Richard Nixon were being intercepted by the Secret Service. More than one hundred people each year reportedly were detained by agents and uniformed officers at the White House during the Nixon administration for making threats or assassination attempts. Many were mentally disturbed.

I found myself undercover again as protests became larger and threats became more frequent and more disruptive. This time on the streets of Washington, I was assigned to a small team of agents charged with ferreting out threats against the president.

The streets were filled with thousands of demonstrators—protesters and veterans against the Vietnam War in the shadow of the Lincoln Memorial, women's libbers fighting for the Equal Rights Amendment, blacks living in tent cities near the Washington Monument, a contingent of Black Panthers, and everyday Americans who wanted their opinions known. Throngs of students were protesting, and we had no idea who they were. The Secret Service Protective Intelligence Division was intercepting multiple threats against the president and other protectees.

Our detail included fellow female agent Phyllis Shantz and another agent from Washington, my buddy Angie from New York, a senior agent from Pennsylvania, and two agents from LA. We lived on the streets and looked like hippies. It was our job to find credible threats in the midst of a political haystack.

We were an interesting group to begin with, even more so after we were sent to the local army surplus store to buy our undercover garb. "Try these," Phyllis said as she peeked her head through army-green jackets and pants. In her hands were bell-bottoms, ripped jeans, and a stack of vests.

I grabbed the striped, hole-ridden pants she pushed my way. She was right, they were ideal. It's strange to look back on my time in the service and realize how young I was. In those fleeting moments of thrift store shopping or a rare night out, we were simply twenty-somethings who laughed about not having boyfriends. But in our case, we didn't have time to date because we were married to our job. Cliché as that is, it's hard to find Prince Charming when you never know whether you'll be flying off to Miami or New York. And much to my mother's dismay, being an agent took priority. I loved my job, as did Phyllis.

"No-shaving pact?" she asked as she stuck out her hand.

My first day undercover as an antiwar hippie, I parted my hair down the middle and wore pigtails. A pair of round gold-rimmed glasses completed my look. My code name was John because I looked like John Lennon. During President Nixon's 1973 inauguration, we were dispatched to the grounds of the Washington Monument. By that time, we were indistinguishable from the hippies; we played the part with the long, stringy hair and dirty backpacks.

In those days, we didn't have sophisticated communication gear—no cell phones or satellite equipment—just a two-way radio. It was imperative we not be discovered as undercover agents. Obviously, carrying a walkie-talkie was a dead giveaway. We had backpacks, but when you're keeping company with hippies, you never know who is going to be rifling through your bag looking for a cigarette or a snack.

"What's the safest place for a radio?" Phyllis asked. "It's too bulky to hide under my jacket."

Just then, genius struck.

We went to a drugstore and bought a big blue box of Kotex and tucked the radio among the white pads. In those days, when Kotex boxes sat on drugstore shelves, they were disguised in brown paper bags. Usually they were behind the counter.

"Why didn't we think of this before? This is the one place no one would dare to look."

"That's brilliant. You should look into a career in law enforcement."

"Not for me," I laughed. "I'd rather be a special agent."

And with that our radio was no longer an issue. When we needed to communicate with the White House staff, we would go to the restroom, pull the radio out of the box that I kept in my backpack, and relay the necessary information. As liberated as those times were, no one looked inside a Kotex box—particularly not men.

These demonstrators were angry, and committed to their goal of disrupting the government. Many were high. They tore down American flags around the Washington Monument, replacing them with Vietnamese flags. They also displayed American flags upside down and eventually burned them. Fires burned in trash cans on the street. We were doing everything we could to protect the first family. Federal troops were sequestered in the White House basement in full riot gear in case the protesters broke the security lines of 1600 Pennsylvania Avenue. And there we stood, between the mayhem and the White House.

It was as anti-American as anything seen today, and it was here at home. From my viewpoint, we were in the midst of a civil war. Even though it was billed as nonviolent, it was still a riot. It was our job to make sure no one got hurt.

We spent hours walking the streets, mingling in the crowds, dodging tear gas, and making ourselves at home at the headquarters of the various "movements." I helped the protesters make signs and edit their antiwar newsletters. As long as we could watch and listen, we were in a great position to find those who were making threats against the president.

We were very busy during the May Day protests as well. I couldn't believe I was in the United States of America. Federal troops in full battle gear with rifles were standing in the doorways of Georgetown shops that carried kites and hand cream. You could see them from President Kennedy's grave site and the eternal flame. Troops lined the Memorial Bridge across the Potomac River and snaked around the Lincoln Memorial. The protesters were doing everything they could to create mass confusion and fear.

Our detail of six was the Secret Service's "flip-flops" on the ground. We assumed many federal agencies were well represented, but we couldn't confirm that. One regular protester, wearing a red construction hat with a peace sign on the front, always played his violin to entertain the crowds until the speakers began. They called him "Henry the Fiddler." I think he worked for the FBI, and I often wondered whether there were as many of them as there were of us.

Today, using advanced countermeasures, the Secret Service executes security operations that identify, deter, minimize, and decisively respond to threats and vulnerabilities. The protective environment is enhanced by specialized resources within the Secret Service, including the Airspace Security Branch, Counter Sniper Team, Emergency Response Team, Counter Surveillance Unit, Counter Assault Team, Hazardous Agent Mitigation and Medical Emergency Response Team, and Magnetometer Operations Unit. Other specialized resources also serve to provide protection from threats including chemical, biological, radiological, and nuclear materials and explosive devices. Today, the Secret Service employs approximately 3,200 special agents, 1,300 uniformed division officers, and more than 2,000 other specialized administrative, professional, and technical support personnel. The team is both diverse and talented.

In the early 1970s, we did the best we could with what we had. And it worked. Under our watch, the president and his visiting foreign dignitaries remained unharmed. Perhaps that makes for a less amusing book, but that means we did our job well.

20

Destructive Ducks

ONE AFTERNOON I was reviewing a check fraud case at WFO when I got a call from Protective Intelligence. "We need you to report to our office. We have a special assignment for you."

Arriving at the Protective Intelligence Headquarters, I was briefed on a current threat. "This guy is crazy!" the agent in charge began.

That was pretty standard. It's said that 70 percent of the threats received against the president were made by those suffering from mental illness. However, this particular plan to kill the president was one of the most bizarre I'd ever heard. "He believes there are underground canals beneath the White House. He plans to make yellow ducks out of plastic explosives," the agent in charge continued. "He intends to rig them with igniters and use his cigar to light them after he's released them and they are floating under the White House."

This radically unstable guy was searching for someone to show him how to execute his plan. Remarkably, the recipes to make these deadly explosives from common household supplies were readily available. The explosives were essentially plastic and could be molded into any form, even yellow ducks.

"Yellow ducks?" I asked, laughing.

"He likes pretty girls, so Clark is going to be our best bet at getting in on his plot. Take her to the lab and give her a quick lesson on the joy of cooking plastic explosives in your kitchen sink. Not the whole deal—this guy is a dope. But undercover she'll need to convince him she's got a source for the goods and knows how to make stuff out of it," he stated.

I nodded enthusiastically.

"Be careful, Clark. It's extremely volatile and very dangerous. If he has any of it at the meet stay away from it."

Nowadays I imagine you can get the recipe on the internet. In the 1970s, I was told you could learn how to make bombs and how to butcher pigs, essentially a "how to" in killing police officers. In the lab, one of the techs gave me a quick course on how to make the stuff and then mold it into what looked remarkably like a rubber duck.

At that point I had enough background, so we set up the meeting. My partner and I pulled up to an abandoned farmhouse in Virginia. I'd been undercover on the streets, so I looked the part.

I was a good student. The perp believed that I had the materials he needed and offered to buy them. As the deal went down he told us his plan and his intent to harm the president. Even if what he said he was going to do was delusional, he had threatened the life of the president, which is against federal law. We made the arrest, cuffed him, and transported him to St. Elizabeth's Psychiatric Hospital in the district.

21

Femmes Fatales

OUR HOUSE on Forty-Fourth Street was getting a little crowded. Four of us were bunking in one bedroom. If two is company and three is a crowd, four is just plain overwhelming.

I decided it was time to move on, and in this case, that meant it was time to move out. Ponce Andres Gebhart and I rented a little one-bedroom apartment on Wisconsin Avenue just down from the Zebra Lounge, across from the National Cathedral. Ponce and I had been friends since college; she'd followed me to Washington and I'd helped her get a job with a Colorado senator. We couldn't afford a two-bedroom apartment, so we shared a room. Breaking glass ceilings didn't pay much.

We were classy, though. Thrifty, yet fashionable. We outfitted our room with two old-fashioned iron beds painted white with brass trim. It was cute and cozy, furnished from yard sales and junk stores, not unlike most apartments single girls shared in the 1970s. The difference was that ours had my framed Christmas cards from the president and Mrs. Nixon hanging on the wall.

Ponce was not an agent, but a great roommate to have if you were one. She got a kick out of my adventures and always had my back.

One night the phone rang at the office. "Hello, Special Agent Clark."

"Kathy?" Ponce whispered.

"Yes? Ponce? Are you all right?"

Femmes Fatales   113

"There is a guy here who says he is an agent and wants to install a red phone under your bed. Is this for real or should I be scared? He has a badge."

"No," I laughed. "It's okay. I'm working undercover and I need a fake number to give out to people."

"Thank goodness," she laughed, her relief evident in her sudden exhale.

"Sorry to startle you like that. I didn't know they'd be coming by this evening. Oh—and don't answer the phone," I quickly added.

"I definitely won't. Have a good night at work."

"Thank you. By the way, my undercover name rhymes with Clark in case you make a mistake. Just don't acknowledge me if we ever meet in public," I stated.

"Of course it does. 'Night," she concluded.

Ponce agreed to all the strange chaos. She and I remain friends today.

Later, Ponce moved back to Colorado, and Denise Ferrenz, the sixth woman admitted to the Secret Service, moved in. We both carried guns in shoulder holsters, so at night we just hung them on the bedposts. Luckily for us, we never had any intruders. Perhaps I should say it was lucky for any burglars they never came into our place. I would like to have seen the look on an intruder's face when two girls in nightgowns drew down on him screaming, "Federal agents, don't move!"

We were safe and we were happy in our Wisconsin Avenue apartment. As is the case in most big cities, the four surrounding blocks of the neighborhood became our world. A short block away there was a dry cleaner, a small grocery store, and a Woolworth variety store that carried a little bit of everything. The highlight of the block was the Zebra Lounge, right on the corner. It was smoky and cramped, with overused fake red leather booths. It looked the same day or night. The interior was always dark, and the only light was that emitted from a handful of neon beer signs. Being an agent didn't afford us much free time, but when we did have a few hours to spare, the Zebra Lounge was our go-to pizza joint for a bite and a cold beer.

It was the day of the vending machine, and the Zebra had two. The first one dispensed condoms: pink ones, ribbed ones, long ones, bigger than you will ever need ones, ones that looked liked a pickle. I had never seen a condom before—let alone hanging in a vending machine in a women's bathroom. For a single quarter, you too could take the first step to free love. Not exactly classy, but definitely progressive. I never did see a condom up close after that.

The cigarette vending machine by the cash register also intrigued me. It was stacked with packs of every brand one could wish for. In 1970 everyone—yes, even women—smoked. Smoking was considered sexy and liberating; it also had the added benefit that it would keep you from eating. Thus, skinny girls were scared that if they quit smoking they would gain weight. They would rather die. Back then, no one thought that smoking was putting them at risk of just that. There were no health alerts on the boxes of the cigarettes of choice for women, Virginia Slims. Virginia Slims are narrower than standard cigarettes (hence, "Slims") and are also longer than normal "king-sized" cigarettes to give them a more "elegant" appearance and purportedly to reduce the amount of smoke produced. Their entire advertising campaign was directed at young women. Oh, how the times have changed.

Having an agent for a roommate had benefits other than pizza nights. Denise and I were both assigned to the foreign dignitary detail protecting Israeli prime minister Golda Meir during her state visit. The special agent in charge, Jerry Parr, told us we would be working the state dinner at the White House the day we were to attend the event.

In those days, there were no guidelines on what we were to wear to formal functions. What to wear was a real problem for women agents. Bottom line, we had to fit in and look like we belonged, yet we had to be able to access our weapons and physically react to any scenario. Today, female agents wear tuxedos like the men. In the early days of the service, they hadn't addressed that issue, and we were on our own. After all, the prime minister was in charge of the Israeli government, and we would be accompanying her to the White House, so we both did our best to dress appropriately. We got ready in our tiny spot. Denise looked beautiful—more like a starlet than a bodyguard. I paled in comparison but made an attempt at state dinner fashion on a minimal budget.

We took our positions at the entrance to Blair House to escort Prime Minister Golda Meir across Pennsylvania Avenue to the White House. Jerry Parr introduced us to her, explaining that we were among the first women the Secret Service had assigned to protect foreign dignitaries. Golda Meir was very cordial, but somewhat dumbfounded.

The prime minister was an elderly woman whose style was sensible at best. She sported black lace-up shoes, a simple gray suit, and stockings rolled just below her knee and tied in a knot. She wore no makeup, and her unruly gray hair was pulled into a bun. All the same, it didn't matter. She was brilliant and one of the world's most important leaders.

Luckily for us, she had a delightful sense of humor. After looking at Denise and me, she said something along the lines of "So what am I in this equation? Chopped liver?"

I later learned she had spent some of her teen years growing up in Denver, Colorado. We might have had more in common than I thought. That's one of the most intriguing parts of working alongside important people; you learn that we all have stuff in common. Dignitaries and diplomats could not do what they do without protection. I may not have been making laws or changing the world, but I was defending the people who were. My contribution was protection and service, and I am honored to have contributed in some small way.

Denise was the only other agent I lived with, but the six of us did work closely with one another. Phyllis and I were frequently paired together. She was tall, with coal-black shoulder-length hair and bangs that got tangled in her eyelashes. Always daring, she wore skirts above her knees—even at our swearing-in ceremony. Despite her beauty, her Jersey accent made her sound tough, and she was. She had an attitude. Phyllis was a good cop, an excellent Secret Service agent, and a great friend.

"Phyllis, what do I do if I ever really get into trouble?" I once asked. "Life or death trouble."

"When I was working at the police station on Capitol Hill, I had a sergeant who didn't like me very much. He enjoyed giving me the midnight shift by myself."

"Why didn't he like you?"

"I'm not sure, to be honest. Maybe because I'm a woman. Maybe because he knew I'd end up a special agent, and he's stuck at sergeant," she answered, smiling mischievously. "Anyways, some rough types in the neighborhood got wind of my lone shift and thought it would be funny to gang up on me."

"What did you do?" I asked.

"You have to look for one of them who is hanging back—not really sure that he wants to do it," she replied. "Just as they circled me to have a little fun, I spotted one reticent kid. I threw him the keys to the squad car parked outside and told him to call in on the radio 'officer down.' He did and another car came to my rescue."

"He actually did it?" I inquired.

"Most of the time you have to act like you're not scared," Phyllis said. "Even when you are—especially when you are."

I stated, "Do it scared. That's what my father used to say."

"When you're scared is when you have to think the most clearly—and you will."

22

Cigs and Sleep Shirts

IN 1972, it was Miami Beach's turn to host both the Democratic and Republican Conventions. President Richard M. Nixon was running for reelection, along with his vice president, Spiro Agnew. Antigovernment protesters were increasing in number and their marches were getting angrier. Threats against the president had spiked. The detail's job in Miami was the same as in Washington, gathering protective intelligence.

Dressed in our hippie attire, we mingled with as many people as we could. The smell of marijuana cigarettes was always in the air at demonstrations and antiwar meetings. Since pot was illegal, smoking a joint was a rite of passage for protesters and was considered a good way to ferret out "pigs." They'd pass a joint in a circle to see who wouldn't smoke. Phyllis and I were always together, so even if we got caught in a circle we worked out a routine where we would hold the joint tight to our lips and act as though we were smoking. Neither of us would inhale and the other agent could corroborate that we hadn't. It was all part of the act.

Pot wasn't the only thing smoked on the streets. The hippie hello was "Can I bum a cigarette?" Angie smoked and always carried a pack in the early undercover days. As the war waged on, the mooching made him so mad he started smoking a corncob pipe. "You look like an old frump smoking a pipe," I told him.

"I'm not giving those goddamned hippies any more cigs," he harrumphed.

When I brought Angie along to some antiwar meetings, I received funny looks. "Why are you hanging around with that old guy smoking a pipe?" girls would ask.

"Oh, he's rich," I would laugh. "And he's really good in bed."

The reality was, I didn't know whether either statement was true, but it was an answer well received in the free-love hippie movement.

Four of us worked the streets at the national convention. Early one morning we took our clothes to a laundromat. While our clothes dried, we went to have breakfast. When we returned, we found that our laundry was missing. These hippies had no idea they'd just stolen the laundry of four armed federal agents.

We launched a full advance, implementing all our training. We conducted interviews with witnesses at the laundromat and tracked down the thieves. One agent stood guard at the back door and one stood at the perimeter of the property as Phyllis and I knocked on the door.

"We think you stole our laundry," Phyllis blurted out as the door opened.

"I didn't steal your laundry," the overweight hippie retorted.

We pushed our way into the apartment and performed a thorough search. Thinking we were street hippies, he didn't protest greatly. Phyllis charged out of the bathroom with the contraband in hand. She'd located one of my sleep shirts that was covered in cats and said, "I bet you don't sleep in a kitty shirt."

With that, we seized the rest of our property and sprinted from the apartment. It was fun, but I'm not sure it was what the Secret Service had in mind when training us with techniques to save the president.

23

Welcome to Miami

"THEY PROBABLY don't believe in paying the light bill," I muttered as I pulled a stack of cheap white paper from the tired copy machine. The pamphlets were printed with hate aimed at the president of the United States. It made me cringe to hold leaflets slandering the very man I'd pledged to protect. My partner, Special Agent Phyllis Shantz, and I had been camped out at the antiwar protesters' headquarters for weeks. Headquarters was really just a dark, musty old motel somewhere in Miami. Spilled wine had clearly stained the pea-green shag carpet, right alongside a cigarette burn mark from a passed-out smoker. Worn faux-wood paneling covered the walls and looked significantly better than the tattered antiwar posters that had been hung with a combination of dirty tape and rusty thumbtacks.

From the small back room stacked floor to ceiling with handouts and posters, I heard angry screams.

"Pig! You're a pig!"

"I don't know what you're talking about," Agent Phyllis Shantz coolly responded.

"You're a pig and you know it. Pig, get out!"

Part of my job was to always have my partner's back. I threw down my copies and stormed into the next room, which was really more of a closet, to find Sheila, a leader in Miami's antiwar movement, and Phyllis, my partner, squared off. The latter had clearly been interrogated by this powerhouse of a woman for some time. She remained calm, but I could see she was concerned.

"What is this all about?" I screamed at Phyllis's vicious challenger.

"You're driving a car that has Dade County Sheriff's Department plates," Sheila accused, jamming her fingers in my face. "You're both pigs!"

The startling part of the allegation being thrust in our faces was that we were, in fact, driving a beat-up T-bird from the Sheriff's Department's impound lot.

Dressed in striped holey pants and an army-green jacket, with unwashed hair parted down the middle, I looked the part of a women's-libber-antiauthority-hippie. Phyllis's unshaved legs told the same story, but what Sheila claimed was true—we were "pigs," if you will—although I preferred to identify myself with the more positive title of US Secret Service agent. We were undercover in Miami Beach, ferreting out threats against President Nixon while he campaigned at the Republican National Convention. But surely they wouldn't have left identifying plates on the car they gave us to drive during an undercover operation.

"Come on," I scoffed. "We're out of here. We just wanted to volunteer to end the war!" Following my lead, Phyllis yelled, "You're the only pig in the room."

Rushing out the back, we pulled open the heavy T-bird doors and jumped into our so-called "undercover" car. I peeled out of the dusty parking lot with my heart racing. "I can't believe Dade County PD screwed us," Phyllis growled.

"Oh well—we've been made," I said. "At least we get to go home."

I whipped the T-bird into the lot by the little bar around the corner, backing into the tight parking space so the plates weren't visible from the street.

"Two vodka martinis, extra cold," I ordered as I slumped onto the bar stool.

"With three cherries each," Phyllis finished.

"Rough day?" the bartender probed.

"We're drinking martinis at two in the afternoon. You could say so."

Grabbing martinis with cherries was kind of our girl thing. It felt feminine, classy, and a bit indulgent.

"Oh, and could I get some quarters?" I asked, placing a five-dollar bill onto the bar top.

Phyllis grabbed the handful of change and headed to the pay phone as I sipped my chilled vodka. Picking at a string, I couldn't help but laugh at my attire. I was grungy. It had taken months to truly look the role, but here I was, looking like a street protester. I always found it puzzling that most people protesting the war wore ragged military castaways. A counterculture, I suppose, likes to strip the military pride in the uniform—deface it and create its own image of the clothing. My amusement turned to frustration as I thought about all the effort Phyllis and I had exerted to blend in, only to have our cover blown by fellow law enforcement.

"He says we have to go back," Phyllis said, shooting her entire drink. She'd just gotten off the phone with the agent in charge of Protective Intelligence. "He says there's no such plates and she's just tooling us. If we don't go back right now, she'll think she nailed us."

So much for going home.

I was scared to death.

But it worked. Sheila apologized when we returned to the protesters' headquarters. This was one of many times I was reminded it was my job to walk directly into the line of fire. Serving as one of the first five female Secret Service agents, I often had to look my fear in the face and do it anyway. To protect and to serve my country required doing it scared, whatever "it" might be, over and over again.

Thousands of antiwar movement protesters during the spring of 1972 in Washington, DC.

Marches grew into larger antiwar protests, and more security was needed to keep control.

Working as an undercover antiwar protester during marches and riots in front of the White House.

Our "Mod Squad" posing as antiwar protesters (left to right): Special Agents Bill Montgomery, Kathryn Clark, and Angie Angelone.

Federal troops and the National Guard were called out to protect the streets of Georgetown during May Day protests in 1972 in Washington, DC.

Working undercover as a hippie.

The portrait *Child in a Straw Hat* by painter Mary Cassatt held a special place in my heart when I moved to Washington and visited the National Art Gallery many times.

Actress Jane Fonda speaking at an antiwar protest during the Republican National Convention, where I worked undercover on the streets in Miami.

Working undercover at an antiwar protest rally.

Special Agent Phyllis Shantz and I used a classic T-bird on loan from the Dade County Police Department for some undercover work in Miami Beach. The very noticeable car almost blew our cover!

Working another protest at the Playboy Club in Miami.

24

The Pistol-Packin' Nanny

MY JOB AS one of the first women to serve my country as a Secret Service agent was supposed to be exciting and high intensity, full of car chases and quick draws of my hidden gun. But the downside of being an agent is that if you're doing your job well, there are no close calls, shootouts, or even subtle disruptions. If we in the service are doing what we're supposed to do, you won't even know we are there. Watching and waiting were an important part of the job, but not particularly exciting. I had been doing a lot of that at the time.

But then my life changed drastically, with a single phone call from Assistant Director Clint Hill.

"In your interview, you said that you could ski, play tennis, and speak German," he said.

"Yes sir," I answered.

"How long would it take for you to get your private life in order for a three-month assignment?"

Private life? I laughed to myself. That didn't exist for young Secret Service agents. Surely he knew that. We gave that up for the people we served and for our country.

"Not long," I quickly responded.

"We're considering assigning you to the KPD," Assistant Director Hill continued.

The KPD! That was the Kennedy children's protective detail. My mind started racing; that would shake things up.

"You will need to meet Mrs. Onassis and the children first."

"Yes sir," I said with a dry throat.

I don't know whether it was routine for an agent to meet with the protectee before being assigned to a detail, but I suppose a children's detail like KPD was anything but typical. As a general rule, first family children don't like having agents around, which can make protecting them quite a challenge. And John and Caroline had never had a woman agent in the mix of their cadre of bodyguards either.

The next day, I flew into Boston's Logan Airport, where the agent in charge met me and said we were going to pick up John at another gate. Although the public referred to the youngest Kennedy as "John-John," family members did not use this nickname. When I tried to visualize John, all I could picture was the three-year-old boy saluting his father's casket in the photo so many Americans recall.

What I expected was an immaculately dressed youngster with a trimmed Beatle-like haircut and pressed khaki pants. The grade-school boy I saw exit the aircraft had eyes obscured by a curly mess of longish brown hair. His khaki pants were unhemmed, worn, and wrinkled. His white shirt had French cuffs held together with bobby pins. Completing the look was a navy-blue blazer that appeared to have doubled as a pillow for the family dog. What I didn't realize was that this disheveled look was considered "preppy" and was common among East Coasters. In fact, all the Kennedy cousins dressed in a similar style—even at a memorial for Robert Kennedy.

We delivered John to Hyannis Port and the Kennedy Compound, where I met his dog and his governess, Marta. The small home looked like any other beach cottage, except a navy trainer airplane, a gift to the president's little boy, sat in the backyard. The plane had no engine, but John told me he loved to pretend he was flying. He was a charming little boy and loved to tell jokes.

At the time, John was eleven years old, and personal freedom wasn't a huge issue. He got along well with his agents and paid little attention to me. He had been surrounded by agents his entire life. My being female did not seem to matter to him. The true test would be when I met with Mrs. Onassis and Caroline. They did not come to Hyannis Port that weekend, and I would have to meet them later.

A week later, I was sent to Hickory Hill, a rolling estate in Virginia, just outside the District of Columbia. A stately two-story traditional southern mansion housed Ethel, Mrs. Robert Kennedy, and her eleven children. When I knocked on the front door, I could hear the giggles of the children, including John and Caroline. None of the Kennedy cousins had ever seen a "girl" agent before. Luckily, I had an ally in winning over the Kennedy children—a young woman my own age named Caroline Croft. She was Mrs. Kennedy's secretary and governess, and she was kind enough to give me the thumbs-up so the cousins appeared to accept me.

Hickory Hill consisted of tennis courts, a swimming pool, lots of grass for football, and a movie room where the brood of children would watch films currently appearing in the movie theaters. This was long before VCRs, DVDs, or movies on demand, so to have one's own movie theater was amazing. One thing that surprised me was that they had their own Coke machine, which had been rigged so a cold soda would come out at the push of a button.

I learned that blending in was important when protecting John and Caroline. Most of the time, I simply "hung around." Hanging around often meant there wasn't much to do. On one of the slower days, Mrs. Ethel Kennedy popped her head around the corner with a paintbrush and can of paint in hand. "Agent Clark? Do you have a moment?"

"Yes, ma'am," I responded quickly.

"Would you mind helping me put a coat of red paint on the front door?"

I couldn't help but chuckle a bit. "Yes, Mrs. Kennedy, maybe I can help."

I'm positive painting wasn't in my job description, but then again, as one of the first women to be a special agent, I was writing my own job description half the time, anyway.

There I was, holding a paintbrush dripping with bright red paint on the front steps of Hickory Hill while protecting two of the most famous children in the world. My college self never saw that coming.

After meeting Caroline at Hickory Hill, I was assigned temporarily to the detail that would accompany her and a band of Kennedy cousins on a shopping trip to Saks Fifth Avenue in New York. At the time, Caroline was fourteen. As with any teenager, friends and freedom from protection were big on her wish list. This trip was a test run, so to speak, and the mission was to buy bathing suits. They packed the elevator with little regard for the older women who also boarded. Teenage girls will be girls—and they were. The women were not impressed and the girls didn't care.

I finally worked my way to the button for the third floor through the rowdy bunch. The doors opened and they spilled out like a pep squad on a yellow school bus. They were teenage girls having fun, but everyone knew they were the Kennedy kids. I was there to keep Caroline safe and happy. "Good luck," I thought to myself.

Things calmed a bit when they dispersed into the racks of brightly colored two-piece numbers. Caroline tried to ignore my presence, and I think she appreciated that I didn't stand out like the male agents in dark suits and earpieces. However, my job remained: create a private, protective barrier for my young protectee.

As Caroline shopped, I stood back and didn't say anything. Consulting on swimwear certainly wasn't covered in my training handbook, but neither were most of the things I ended up doing to keep her safe, happy, and alive. The most important thing was to make her comfortable having me near. That was the only way I could protect her. Caroline decided against buying a swimsuit altogether. She went back to laughing with her friends, and I recognized that that was also my job—even with me tagging along she deserved to have some normalcy, whatever normal was.

When she was in the public eye, people were drawn to Caroline. Like her mother, she was very private and did not enjoy the attention. Admirers of her father were thrilled to see her. I was amazed at how little respect they had for her privacy, as though she were their public property. At fourteen, being in the spotlight was exhausting, not fun. There was nothing I could do but intercede when I could.

Even though many years had passed since President Kennedy's assassination, strangers would approach her and offer condolences. I suppose most had good intentions, but it was intrusive and potentially dangerous. As her agent, I had no idea who they were and whether they presented a threat to her safety. I found out early on that this would be one of the primary things I would have to figure out and handle appropriately. There was more to it than having a loaded gun in your purse.

25

Where in the World Is Scorpios?

A FEW DAYS later another call came from Mr. Hill. "Well, Kathryn," he said. "I guess you passed muster. I am assigning you to the Kennedy children's detail."

Mr. Hill began explaining my assignment. "You will be overseas for two to three months. Depart next week. Meet up with KPD in New York and fly with the children to Paris. There, John and Caroline will join their mother on board Onassis's yacht and sail to Greece with multiple stops along the way."

His laundry list of details continued. "The detail will hop from port to port—Nice, Rome, Athens, Capri, Sorrento, and Pompeii. Protect them when they depart the ship. It's a complicated advance with a lot of planning. The advance is already underway. Final destination is Athens. KPD will be based there, but you will spend most of your assignment on the small island of Scorpios not far from Onassis's private island. You can meet Mrs. Onassis there and set up communications with her. I will notify KPD of your arrival in New York next week and they will bring you up to speed. Do you have any questions at this point?" he asked.

Taking a deep breath, I responded, "No, sir." Asking for questions was more a formality than a genuine interest in my peace of mind.

Three months abroad sounded incredible. Less than a week until I left. Not much lead time. Greece. I'd be staying near a private island. And not just any private island, the island where Mrs. Onassis and her children would be staying. The life of an agent is by no means glamorous—on the contrary, you usually end up tucked away out of sight—but I'd never been to Nice or Rome, and I'd only read about Pompeii and Athens in my history books. Seeing a bit of the world was a nice perk I was very much looking forward to.

Getting my life in order wasn't difficult. I packed a few things, handed my apartment keys to Denise, and picked up my ticket to Paris. The luster was back.

Before I left, I did a little research on my new assignment. The children were slated to spend a month on Scorpios, a private island in the Ionian Sea just off the western coast of Greece, the personal property of their stepfather, billionaire Aristotle Onassis, and the site of his wedding to the former first lady of the United States in 1968. Since their marriage, John and Caroline had visited the island each summer. The KPD consisted of seven men—and now one woman—who were assigned to protect the children. The men rotated in and out of Athens, but I was posted in Nydri, a small village located a short boat ride from Scorpios.

The flight to Paris was first class on Olympic, an airline owned by Mr. Onassis. Because it was an Onassis expectation and not a perk, the service was something else. The protective "port hopping" was uneventful—just like the Secret Service likes it. From a personal perspective, I had never been to the fascinating stops all along the way to Athens.

Once we were settled in an American military officers' hotel in Athens, I was dispatched to my island post in the Ionian Sea. Getting to the small town of Nydri was no easy feat.

To get me to Nydri, one of the agents took me to the American air force base nearby. With little fanfare and few instructions, I climbed aboard a military transport plane as the only passenger. Outfitted with canvas seats along the sides of an empty aluminum body, it looked like the kind of plane they jumped out of in World War II. Unfortunately, I didn't have a parachute.

The ride was bumpy and the roar of the prop engines ear splitting. The open door left a gaping hole in the side of the plane. A bit disconcerting, but it afforded a remarkable view. The sea was as blue as the hills were dry.

After a short flight, the pilot slowed the big engines and landed the old workhorse of a plane on the eastern coast of the island of Lefkada. We touched down on a short dirt runway. Coming to a stop with a storm of

Greek dust swirling around the plane, the pilot gave me a bit of a push out the door and told me to find a taxi. It was a bit more of a jump than I expected.

Over the roar of the engines he hollered, "Tell them you want to go to Nydri."

He gave me a snappy salute, revved up the engines, and took off. It was obvious he thought it beneath him to ferry an unlikely female Secret Service agent around the Greek coast.

There I stood, clutching my bright blue Olympic Airlines flight bag. I had packed light—a couple pairs of shorts, T-shirts, a bathing suit, and my .357 Magnum revolver. No taxi was in sight.

Eventually, a dirty little battered blue car crept around one of the treeless hills surrounding the landing strip. I guess the driver had seen the plane land from the tiny village down the way and had come in hopes of a fare, which in this part of Greece was rare. I spoke no Greek and he spoke no English. Raising both hands palms up, he asked where I wanted to go.

"Nydri," I answered and climbed in.

We crept down the narrow one-way road. I looked down at the ocean below—quite a way below—as the road twisted and turned like a snake. I think I was supposed to feel safe because a plastic statue of the Virgin Mary was taped to the dashboard under red flapper fringe across the windshield. The Greek worry beads hanging from the rearview mirror swayed to the rhythm of the little car. My fingernails dug into the seat as if that could prevent another taxi from careening along the narrow road and launching full force into this tin can called a taxi.

If I was going to die for my country, I certainly hoped it'd be with a bit more purpose than a car accident in Greece. Maybe the Virgin Mary was looking out for me after all, because we arrived in one piece. No one greeted me, but that wasn't surprising. Agents greeted protectees upon arrival, or protectees were greeted by other diplomats or the family members they were traveling to see. Wherever we traveled, we left our loved ones behind.

26

Three Women

THERE WASN'T much to Nydri. It was a tiny village of a few hundred people, visiting fishermen, a couple of donkeys and goats, and, temporarily, one young Colorado girl whom few realized was a United States Secret Service agent. My home that summer was a tiny hotel room with a single light bulb hanging from the ceiling and a communal bath down the hall. It was simple and clean. No luxury here, but it suited me just fine.

Across the Ionian Sea—about five minutes by a sixteen-foot Boston Whaler—I could see the island of Scorpios, and Caroline and John's home aboard the luxurious yacht *Christina*. A tomato-red speedboat named *John* and a two-masted sailboat named *Caroline* bobbed in the marina where the *Christina* was moored. While the children lived on Scorpios, I stayed in Nydri, on call so to speak. My presence wasn't required on Scorpios itself because Mr. Onassis had made the island secure for the children.

The *Christina* was the monarch of the marina. It was more than three hundred feet long and had a crew of thirty-nine, all of whom wore pristine long-sleeved white cotton shirts with CHRISTINA emblazoned on the front. Their white cotton twill pants matched the color of the motor yacht. As my father would say, "She was a dandy big boat."

I had read a bit about the yacht before we arrived. The *Christina* was originally a Canadian antisubmarine river-class frigate launched in 1943 and was present at the D-Day landings. After the war, Aristotle Onassis purchased the ship for its scrap value, approximately US$34,000, and subsequently spent $4 million to convert it into a luxurious yacht, which he renamed *Christina* after his daughter.

My job was to sit on the beach, waiting for a message from Mrs. Onassis when there were plans for Caroline or John to leave the island. She would send one of the crew in a tiny Boston Whaler to fetch me. The first time, a handsome Greek fellow with bulging biceps peeking out of his crew shirt dropped me at the dock. Even though the *Christina* was only 325 feet long, Mr. Onassis had done a lot with his $4 million, and Mrs. Onassis had obviously added her touches.

The gangplank was either teak or mahogany—I can't remember which. Everything wooden gleamed. It was beautiful. The brass fittings shined. Fresh flowers in huge vases stood like sentries on mahogany tables. Paintings by van Gogh, Renoir, and a few others I recognized from my college art history classes hung on the walls. In Ari's Bar, the barstools were upholstered in very soft, fine leather made from whale foreskin. In addition to the master suite, there were eighteen passenger staterooms and numerous indoor and outdoor living areas, all connected by a spiral staircase.

The aft main deck boasted a crisp blue and white Greek flag. There was an outdoor swimming pool with a Greek-themed mosaic floor. With a mere push of a button, the mosaic swimming pool could be drained, raised to deck level, and transformed into a dance floor where a white baby grand piano sat at the ready. Over the years people such as Grace Kelly, Marilyn Monroe, Rudolph Nureyev, Eva Perón, and Frank Sinatra had sailed as guests of the Onassis family. A helicopter platform was on the promenade deck. To say the *Christina* was luxurious would be an understatement.

Truth be told, I had few meetings with Mrs. Onassis. I was on call and spent most of my time in Nydri waiting. In the Secret Service, they call this standing post. Some places are better to stand post and wait than others.

The local folks and fishermen became my friends. The only restaurant was next door to my hotel. The seating area comprised a few metal tables and beach chairs scattered about the bulkhead of the dock and spilling onto a patch of gravel. The arrangement depended on the prior evening's party. A single string of white lights hung precariously from an olive tree, and a pole hosted remnants of what was once a Greek flag. The little café looked straight out of the movie set of *Zorba the Greek*. The restaurant had no name and a limited menu—usually fish soup with eyeballs intact, blood sausage, or goat intestines—but it did have a lot of cheap red or white Domestica wine. A good bottle cost ninety-nine cents. They all cost ninety-nine cents.

Many nights, traditional Greek music blared from a worn stereo playing scratched records late into the night. An old man wearing a navy-blue fisherman's cap with an unkempt white mustache served ouzo in small glasses that were either dirty or well worn. I assumed the latter and drank the ouzo, which tasted strangely like licorice. Sometimes Mr. Onassis would send over a case of Dom Pérignon champagne for the yacht's crew. I felt lucky they befriended me and often invited me to their raucous parties. Plates flew through the air and then crashed to the cement, usually until they ran out of them. It seemed senseless.

In the back of an open-air kitchen, an ancient black-and-white television played reruns of *FBI*, an American television show starring Efrem Zimbalist Jr. Although Zimbalist wasn't Greek—he was from New York and had gone to Yale—the Greeks adopted him as their own, and he had achieved national celebrity status. Having little to do when I was off duty, I watched a lot of FBI arrests in Greek. It came in handy later.

When I wasn't watching reruns, I watched the people and activity in the tiny town. In Greece, all widowed women wore simple black dresses, black shoes, and a black head cover for the rest of their lives. I never heard what happened if they found a new husband. There were a lot of older women in black, so I figured it didn't happen too often.

Most of the undernourished village was in a constant state of construction, but there didn't seem to be much urgency in completing the projects they'd begun. Partially built houses had no indications of a finish date, and humble little homes had few plants and lots of dust. A few wind-weary olive trees dotted the dusty little road that I suppose would be considered the main street. Other than the battered blue taxi that brought me, I saw few cars.

Women swept with brooms made from a bundle of twigs tied in a ponytail-like fashion and attached to a long stick. An occasional donkey was herded down the narrow dirt paths. Everyone on the island drank a lot of very strong coffee and ate small bowls of olives. Every house had a barrel of olives. I didn't much care for the olives, but I was a big fan of the coffee.

I would walk the hills in the afternoon to exercise. One of the older widow ladies befriended me. She invited me to come for coffee several times a week. I would climb up the stairs, and she would greet me with "Yassou" (hello), "Kalimera" (good morning), or "Kalispera" (good evening). That was the extent of our conversation because it was all the Greek I knew.

I would sit down in a small chair in the sparsely furnished living room. Disappearing behind a heavy cotton curtain separating the tiny kitchen from the rest of the house, she would return with a lovely but tiny china cup filled with a strong, thick coffee, and a little bowl of sugar. After one sip, I learned Greek coffee requires a lot of sugar. She would sit next to me, nod at the cup, and pat me on the leg. I would nod back, waiting for her to serve herself. We nodded back and forth for some time. Then it became clear that she wasn't joining me. It became our little ritual.

My three-word vocabulary provided limited conversation, so one day I pulled an American nickel out of my pocket. Pointing to one side, I said "heads" and then flipped it and said "tails." She laughed, and we played the heads or tails game to fill the dead air space. We laughed together and oddly became friends. Being an agent could be lonely—exceedingly lonely at times. I expect being a widow was much the same way. We didn't need to speak to bond; we simply needed to laugh and to be together to enjoy a little fellowship.

Toward the end of my time there, her daughter came to visit from the United States. She spoke excellent English. One night, we sat at the restaurant and shared a bottle of Domestica.

"Why won't your mother drink coffee with me?" I asked.

"She is a proud woman and only has one cup she feels is nice enough to share with you," she replied quietly.

With that, I could understand her refusal to join me. I continued drinking my wine and chatting with her daughter. We talked of pop culture and why she'd moved to the United States, what she wanted to do with her life, and what it was like to be an agent in the United States Secret Service.

As my assignment in Nydri came to a close, I reflected on how interesting my life was. Some afternoons I met with former first lady of the United States Jacqueline Kennedy Onassis aboard a multimillion-dollar yacht, and other times I drank coffee with a proud but unassuming Greek widow in her unfinished tiny home, from her favorite cup. Quite a juxta-position of lifestyles, yet the two women had one thing in common—they were both widowed at a young age, living their lives as best they could relative to what life had dealt them.

27

Joining the FBI

THE ONLY time standing post wasn't somewhat monotonous was when I was sitting on the beach in Greece. While Caroline's summer plans were made, I lay in the Mediterranean sun. That was before the fear of skin cancer, so I felt no remorse.

One afternoon while sunbathing/standing post, I saw a boat coming toward the dock. Not having cell phones meant Mrs. Onassis sent messages via the *Christina*'s crew. Like many American moms, the most famous mother in the world was planning her daughter's activities, which included an Austrian tennis camp and a skiing camp, so it appeared my time in Nydri had concluded.

When I boarded the *Christina*, I was greeted by Mrs. Onassis, who was wearing a pink and white checkered two-piece bathing suit, with no makeup and no sunglasses. She briefed me on Caroline's upcoming itinerary. I would be ensuring her daughter's safety while working undercover at various summer camps in Mayrhofen, Austria.

Several days later, the same dusty blue taxi that had taken me to Nydri reappeared. When we arrived at the tiny airport on the next island over, people were waiting in a long line beside a white tent by the makeshift departure building. In those days, Greek security was much stricter than ours.

An imposing matron with a badge of some sort was bellowing in Greek at passengers to open their bags. Some women were being culled from the line for strip searches in the back of the tent. Clearly, she would not be happy when she found a weapon in my flight bag.

I thought these officials would acknowledge my gold badge and commission book, which stated in English that I was on a mission for the president of the United States as a Secret Service agent. No problem, I thought. I will just flash the badge and avoid the confrontation.

Well, that didn't work. She grabbed the handles of my bag and began to unzip it, paying no attention to my credentials.

"Secret Service," I explained again and again. "Protection—Caroline Kennedy!"

Passengers boarded the small plane. The propellers were blowing dust and billowing the sides of the tent where the matron was intent on searching my bag and strip-searching me. Out of desperation and pure luck, I remembered the revered actor Efrem Zimbalist Jr.

"I work for the FBI with Efrem Zimbalist in America!" I screamed, while pounding my chest.

Luckily an English-speaking police officer understood, grabbed her arm, and said with raised eyebrows and admiration, "Oh—FBI, FBI."

She looked at me with a mix of intrigue and disgust. Gingerly, I pulled the handles of my flight bag from her grasp and ran to the plane, pushing my way into the cabin. The other passengers had heard the confrontation and didn't say a word.

If I was FBI, then I was somebody, and now I was on my way to Austria.

28

The Karate Lady Loves Geraniums

MY TYPING classes weren't necessary for attending summer camp in the Austrian Alps with a fourteen-year-old celebrity. My high school extracurricular activities, however, proved useful. My assignment: accompany Caroline on all her exploits throughout Mayrhofen, Austria. My unspoken mission: ensure Caroline Kennedy was safe, alive, and happy, while keeping her from dishonoring the former president of the United States and her famous mother. That's not exactly how it was phrased in the handbook, but it was my reality.

Every morning, I would warm her up for her tennis lesson. My Olympic Airlines flight bag with my "equipment" tucked inside sat near the baseline of the court. In the afternoon, I strapped on my skis and followed her down the mountain. For all intents and purposes, I was an undercover camp counselor. Few people knew what I really did.

The paparazzi were driving both Caroline and me crazy. They dangled from the trees and buildings around the tennis courts waiting for the photo op that they hoped would embarrass the teenager. They were not threatening her life, but they were making her unhappy.

Early in the first week, my cover was blown. I'm not entirely sure what events transpired that exposed me as more than a ski instructor, but it was the best thing that could have happened. One afternoon, Caroline and I were walking down Mayrhofen's cobblestoned streets on our way to get an ice-cream cone. The photographers were in hot pursuit.

Small newsstands dotted the main square. I noticed the front page of the German version of the *National Enquirer* prominently displayed. In a font large enough to announce the end of World War II, the banner headline read "Mit Tennisschläger und Karate-Dame." Translation: Caroline had been seen "With Tennis Racket and Karate Lady." The article said that the famous Kennedy youngster was in town attending a tennis camp—along with her bodyguard, the "Karate Lady." I hoped readers—including the irritating paparazzi—would infer that I could kill a man with my bare hands and was likely to do so if people didn't leave her alone. When we saw them, I usually turned around and gave them my best "special agent stare," hoping they would recognize me. To my surprise, it worked and the paparazzi kept their distance—at least for a day or two.

I had begun to believe I enjoyed my career so much I didn't need a personal life. Then one afternoon after several ski runs behind Caroline, I met a bright, handsome man.

"You're pretty good out there," he said.

"I have to keep up with my campers," I replied, stumbling over my words.

"Campers, huh? You're a counselor?"

"You could say that. I'm Kathryn, by the way."

"Fritz," he said as he smiled, extending his cold hand in my direction. "Do camp counselors get days off?"

"Sometimes," I ventured.

"Well next time you do, you should come by for a glass of schnapps."

"What's that?"

"Are you American?"

I nodded.

"It's an Austrian fruit liquor—potent and thick. Like a brandy after-dinner drink."

"I'd very much like that."

And with that, I agreed to my first date in what seemed like years. The details are ensconced in a schnapps haze, but the first date must have gone well, because I spent each and every off-duty afternoon cuddling on his couch. In the Austrian Alps it generally rains in the late afternoon. I loved listening to the raindrops plopping off the roof of his tiny chalet and watching the red geraniums bounce in the brightly painted window boxes when the rain made contact. We'd play classical music on his record player and talk with candor about what we hoped the future held. He was more certain than I of what he wanted and where he was headed. It was hard for me to imagine my own life when my professional life was so focused on the lives of my protectees.

My afternoons with Fritz were a lovely interlude in my otherwise lacking personal life. But as with all my assignments, my time in Austria ended and I moved on. Those afternoons did get me thinking, though. Was there a different path for me that included a few geraniums and raindrops?

29

Protection in Unusual Places

CAROLINE WAS much like her mother in style and demeanor. She was often quiet and subdued but could be funny when she cracked that Kennedy smile. She was insightful and bright. She always looked cute, even if she was no frills. She wore her curly sun-streaked hair shoulder length and pulled it back in a ponytail. She was blessed with lots of beautiful hair. She frequently wore a Diane von Furstenberg wraparound dress and slip-on loafers.

Passionate about photography, she carried a big Nikon with a long lens across her shoulder in lieu of a purse or handbag.

For the most part, I think she appreciated the Secret Service even though she didn't like it. In some cases, our presence was quite convenient. We would drive her places, and she liked that. On the other hand, she found having someone around all the time inhibitive to her already limited teenage freedom. I hope having me in her shadow was a little easier than it would have been being trailed by more obvious male agents.

Once in a while, she did admit, I came in handy. Once on a flight to Boston I was sitting with her in first class when she went to the restroom. If she had been the first lady, I would have stood post outside the door, but I was trying to be less intrusive with her. I kept my eye on the door from my seat and waited. And waited. And waited.

After what seemed like a very long time, I walked down the aisle and knocked on the door.

"Are you okay?" I asked.

"Where have you been?" she whispered, obviously embarrassed and a little irritated. "The door is broken and I can't get out."

I jumped into action. I was highly trained, but not for this situation—so I called the flight attendant. She couldn't get it open either. By now, everyone in first class knew that the passenger who looked like Caroline Kennedy was, in fact, Caroline Kennedy. We pulled the copilot, who had a key, from the cockpit. The plane full of passengers cheered when she finally emerged from the bathroom. Both of us were a little embarrassed.

Bathrooms could be a problem. In Austria, she and all the kids from the camp in Mayrhofen went to the opera in Salzburg. As the lights came down, Caroline decided to exit the hall.

I followed, along with a male agent and four Austrian security officers who had come along. As we all exited into the empty lobby, Caroline turned around and said, "Please, can I just go to the bathroom?"

"You guys return to your posts in the hall," I instructed the others. "I'll wait for her here."

A couple of the security officers turned around and immediately started walking in the other direction. The other two looked concerned. "I've got this," I assured them.

I waited outside the restroom, not anticipating any drama. All was well until I heard a heated discussion through the door—some in English and some in German. I entered the bathroom and found a furious bathroom attendant haranguing Caroline. Through my two years of high school German, I gathered that the tradition, and therefore the expectation, in Austria was to put a few coins in a dish for the attendant before using the stall.

"Did you pay the lady, Caroline?" I asked kindly. I wasn't accusing her, just trying to defuse the situation.

"No," she said. "I don't have any money on me."

Luckily, I did. I paid the woman and rescued my charge.

"Thank you," Caroline whispered as I escorted her from the ladies' room.

"What good is a special agent if she can't get you out of a bathroom every now and again?"

I laughed at my own joke. Caroline eventually cracked a smile.

30

Do You Have an Aspirin?

SURROUNDED BY sparkling lights and tinsel, I paused from hanging ornaments on my tiny tree to answer the ringing phone. I'd always loved Christmas, and although being on the Kennedy protective detail ensured that I was going to have to work this holiday season, I was determined to cultivate some yuletide cheer. As I was humming along with the fa-la-las, the phone rang. "Hello!" I answered joyfully. I was a girl close to her midtwenties living on her own in Washington, DC, with her very own Christmas decorations.

"Agent Clark?" the agent in charge asked.

"Speaking," I replied.

"The family will be spending the holidays in England with Mrs. Onassis's sister. We will depart day after tomorrow."

"Yes sir, Merry Christmas," I said.

"And Clark? Be prepared for a fox hunt on horseback and a pheasant shoot."

Sometimes laughter was the only way to make sense of the craziness I signed up for. I packed accordingly—a pair of tweed slacks, boots, and a leather jacket. "That will have to do," I muttered as I zipped up my suitcase.

Forty hours later, Caroline, John, Marta, the governess, and I landed at London's Heathrow Airport just before dawn. We disembarked from the Olympic Airlines plane. A Rolls-Royce Silver Cloud was waiting on the runway to carry us and the rest of the detail to Henley-on-Thames, the country home of Polish émigré nobleman Prince Stanislas "Stash" Radziwill, the husband of Mrs. Onassis's sister.

Veteran Secret Service agent Muggsy O'Leary was on this trip as well. He was dressed in a tweed overcoat, circa 1945, and his ever-present gray fedora. Muggsy was quite a sight with a stubby cigar jammed in the corner of his mouth and no teeth. What a character he was! In his late seventies, he looked even older; his kind face had lost its shape because he rarely wore his dentures. Nothing about Muggsy or his demeanor suggested he was the agent among us with the most seniority and the one who had open access to the former first lady. In fact, Muggsy always called her by her first name.

Muggsy was an urban legend in the agency. His real name was John J. O'Leary. He had been a Capitol Hill police officer for years. When Muggsy was a young man, Congressman Jack Kennedy hired him as his bodyguard and driver. It was said that JFK carried Muggsy's dentures in the pocket of his overcoat and would insist that he wear them on special occasions. As the story goes, President Kennedy called the director of the Secret Service and instructed him to have Muggsy sworn in as a special agent for life.

Special Agent O'Leary pushed infant Caroline's pram when she left the hospital, and he was on the detail the day President Kennedy was assassinated. Muggsy had a history with the Kennedys, and that's why he was there. The people the Secret Service protect are not always up front about their plans. Perhaps they found it intrusive, but it made it more difficult for us to protect them. Muggsy never had that problem. Mrs. "O" trusted him. He had access to her plans and those of the children.

A good Irish Catholic boy, Muggsy hailed from South Boston. He was known as "Southey," yet another endearing nickname. He always added multiple *a*'s and *ah*'s to every word he spoke. Not only was he bigger than life, but his accent was legendary as well.

"Claaaark," he'd call me. "Jaaaackie," he'd called Mrs. Onassis. For some reason Muggsy took a liking to me, and we became great friends. Although we made an odd team, the special agent in charge usually assigned us to work together. It became clear that part of my job was to take care of Muggsy as well as the Kennedys. Oddly, he thought he was taking care of me. He was always concerned about me. One day he asked me to carry his old Colt .45 from his Capitol Hill days in my already-packed purse. He told me it was too heavy. So I carried it, disguising my gratefulness for his concern with a charade of ignorance and helpfulness.

Once I asked him whether he had any children. "No, Claaaark," he said, "But I don't throw any bricks in any schoolyaaaard." To this day, when someone asks me whether I ever had children, I hear Muggsy's voice in my head. I was lucky enough to have my own son and three stepchildren, but many agents were not so lucky.

When we landed at Heathrow I had a headache, but we had no time to stop at a drugstore. "Do you have a couple of aspirin?" I asked as we climbed into the Rolls-Royce.

"No, Claaaark," he said. "But I'll take care of ya."

With the time change, it was early morning by the time we arrived at the Radziwell estate. The sun was rising behind what looked like a classic English castle with a large entrance and driveway. The car's tires made a rich crunching sound on the gravel as we pulled to a stop.

Down the lane, I noticed a woman jogging toward us. Her hair was covered with a cotton scarf, and despite the early morning she wore large sunglasses. "Oh no," I thought. "That's Mrs. Onassis!" Here I was, disheveled and exhausted. So many times I had dressed the part and was ready to interact as the agent protecting her children. This was not one of those moments.

"Hey, Jaaaackie!" called Muggsy as she approached us. "Agent Claaaark here has a headache. Ya got any aspirin?"

He wasn't wearing his dentures, but it didn't seem to matter. Mrs. Onassis smiled and disappeared into the house, returning with two tiny pills wrapped in tissue. I thanked her and slipped them into my pocket. It was awkward. Muggsy thought nothing of it. He was used to being around the Kennedys.

31

On Duty, but Invisible

CHRISTMAS WAS not the best of times to be a Secret Service agent. I was a long way from family and home. On Christmas Eve and Christmas Day, Muggsy and I sat in a small room off the main dining room as the family celebrated. They brought us dinner, but the reality of standing post, including its unglamorous aspects, was part of the job. We were invisible, and Christmas is not a great time to be invisible. Muggsy had spent many nights like this. We had volunteered to stand post because the other agents had brought their wives, so they got the night off.

The next morning, the SAIC handed me a stack of passports and said Caroline was going fox hunting in York, England. I was to go with her while the rest of the detail would stay with John Kennedy Jr. at Henley. I was charged with taking care of the travel arrangements and security as well as the entire hunting party's passports. I chuckled a bit as I flipped through the documents. One belonged to Prince Radziwell. Under occupation, it said simply "Gentleman." Who knew? I always wondered what royals did.

After getting everyone settled on the train, I began to wonder how I would guard Caroline while she was chasing an elusive fox. What if I didn't have a horse!

As I surveyed the gathering of red-coated huntsmen surrounded by a pack of handsome beagles, I noticed a group of scruffy grooms hanging back around a muddy green vehicle. The Land Rover smelled like a stable and the floor looked like one. "Secret Service," I said, flipping open my badge and black commission book. No one said anything. I just received blank stares.

"I need to keep up with Caroline Kennedy. Seems they forgot my horse, so do you think I could ride along with you fellows?" I asked, laughing.

"Sure thing, my lady," one of them said, pushing aside extra gear and muddy boots to make room for me. It was a bumpy ride, but we kept up. Caroline didn't fall off the horse or catch the fox. All in all, it was a successful day of protection. Nothing bad happened.

The next day was a pheasant hunt that would have done PBS's *Downton Abbey* proud. The men, including Winston Churchill's grandson, were decked out in the tweed of the day. Loaders, who carried matched sets of over-and-under Purdey shotguns, accompanied each shooter. Spaniel retrievers stood at attention at the side of their handlers as fifty or so townsfolk, serving as "beaters," walked through the woods hollering and waving sticks in the brush to drive the birds toward the regal participants.

As the birds flew, a shooter would take aim and shoot. If he missed, the loader would hand him a second gun, ready to go. After all the shots were fired, the dogs were released to retrieve the birds. A covered horse-drawn wagon stood by. The pheasants were hung by their necks, loaded into the wagon, and taken back to the village, where they were given to the poor. Caroline just watched, and I watched her. I was glad they didn't ask me to shoot—I might have embarrassed the agency. I am not good with shotguns.

Following the hunt, a formal lunch, complete with starched white linens, silver, china, and crystal, was served in a small greenhouse in a clearing in the woods. I'm sure the main dish must have been pheasant under glass. Luckily for me, I didn't have to eat with the loaders and handlers. I just had to act as though I had done this many times. Protection wasn't that different from undercover work.

32

T-boned on First Avenue

MOST OFTEN, I was assigned to the Kennedy protective detail when the children were traveling, but occasionally the detail would bring me from Washington to protect Caroline in New York City, where their apartment was located on Fifth Avenue. On those occasions, I would accompany her to the Brearley School, a private institution in midtown Manhattan.

Mischief sometimes raised its ugly head during those times. On some days, Caroline preferred to ride the city bus or walk to school with her friends. Can you imagine how difficult it was to follow her bus in the sea of buses on Fifth Avenue and then try to keep up with her as she walked down a busy street? One day, she and her friends decided it would be funny to walk the wrong way down a one-way street. All I could do was follow them down the block, then throw the red light on top of the car, hit the siren, and drive around the block to catch up with them on the other side. Anywhere but New York I would have looked like an idiot.

By the time we got to the school, I was angry. As I pulled up to the steps behind Caroline and her friends, I motioned to her.

"What's wrong?" she asked.

"Hey kiddo, I can't take this kind of stuff," I said. "I don't mind a little fun now and then, but I'm not going to lose you on my watch. Would you rather have the big guys with the dark glasses back?"

She laughed and I couldn't help but join her. She never did that to me again. Most of the time she acted like I wasn't there and I pretended I wasn't. That arrangement worked just fine for both of us.

Then there was the day after school when she jumped in the car, threw her book bag on the floor, and said, "I have to tutor today, and we are *late.*"

"Where?" I said. "It's not on your schedule."

"Oh, it's across town—just up First Avenue," she replied and told me how to get there.

"Okay," I said, pulling away from the curb.

I radioed our change of plans back to the command post. After a few minutes, without warning, she yelled, "Turn here! Turn here!" Keep in mind that First Avenue is a busy six-lane street with a large center island. Luckily, I was in the left-hand lane. There was no oncoming traffic, so I took the turn.

Instantly, I felt a crash as another vehicle T-boned ours. "Get down on the floor and stay down," I screamed at Caroline.

Pulling my gun from my shoulder holster, I jumped from the car expecting the worst. I had just completed a special defensive driving course in Washington a few weeks prior dealing with this kind of attack, and my mind was racing with all the possible scenarios. Not one was positive.

Alone with Caroline, I was quite certain this was a kidnapping scenario. I scanned the rooftops and swung around in a full circle to survey what I was facing. Through steam streaming from under the hood of a finned 1962 Cadillac with prior damage patched with Bondo, I saw my assailant. The driver was a sixty-two-year-old white male with a big belly, wearing a porkpie hat. He had a little cigar jammed in the corner of his mouth and chubby, unshaven cheeks.

Remembering what I had learned in training—if it doesn't look right, it probably isn't—I felt that something didn't fit this scenario. Yet I wasn't sure what might happen next, so I reholstered my weapon, stood down a bit, caught him up short, and pushed him over the hood of the car.

"Secret Service! Secret Service! You're under arrest!" I yelled.

I glanced back and saw Caroline peering through the back window. "Get down, get down," I yelled while struggling to subdue my unlikely assailant.

"Lady, lady," he mumbled and kept trying to say something. Then I understood.

"You hit me! You hit me. Ya pulled right out in front a me. This here is a one-way street!" he exclaimed. A look at the traffic creeping around our accident confirmed that he was right.

Neither vehicle had much damage. Mustering my best smile, I dusted him off, patted his hat back in place, and handed him one of my business cards.

"Sorry about this, sir," I said with all the confidence I could muster. "Call this number, and the Secret Service will take care of any damage to your beautiful Cadillac."

Somehow the charm worked, and he toddled away, still chomping on his cigar. I slid back into the car. Caroline looked at me with wide eyes.

"You're pretty good," she said. "I'll bet you scared him to death."

I laughed and said, "Next time, give me a little more lead time on the left turns. Okay?"

Caroline arrived late, but in one piece, to her tutoring session, which gave me a solid hour to stress over the repercussions of my little T-bone incident. I was slightly worried the higher-ups would give me grief because it was my fault, but more concerned that the men would make fun of me. "You hit me, you hit me," rang in my head. I was horrified. There goes your reputation of being able to handle yourself, I thought. That's the downfall of being a pioneering woman in any field; there is no room for error. You not only have to do what the men do; you must do it better, without displaying too much effort. As a woman, I had to constantly defend my right to be there. That's a big pill to swallow in your midtwenties.

When I returned to Washington, there was no mention of my accident. No reprimands or mockery. I was relieved.

33

It Never Hurts to Ask for Directions

WHEN WE were assigned to the Kennedy protective detail in New York, our job was to be out of sight but at the ready. In other words, invisible in the lives of the people we were protecting. We worked out of a tiny command post on Fifth Avenue, basically an oversized closet with three battered chairs and one dirty window overlooking a dirty alley. In the same building, Mrs. Onassis had an apartment overlooking Central Park.

One evening, a call came that Mrs. Onassis and Caroline needed an agent to take them to Rockefeller Center. I had worked undercover in the city and had been assigned there several times, but I was still unaccustomed to driving.

With the same crooked smile I had seen before outside Mrs. Mitchel's door, one of the men threw me the keys and chided, "Here, Clark. You drive them."

A little panicky, I grabbed the jingling keys in midair without a word. I walked toward the black government sedan and waited by the door. Mrs. Onassis and Caroline emerged from the building. I could see the men watching from behind the doorman. I slid behind the steering wheel and toward Mrs. Onassis, thinking this would probably be my last day in the Secret Service.

"Mrs. Onassis," I said with a bit of a laugh, "you will not believe this, but I could use your help. The men on the detail have set me up, so to speak. They know I am not familiar with New York. I was wondering if you would mind giving me directions to your destination?"

"Oh, my," she said in her lovely whispering voice, "that's amusing. Men don't like to ask for directions, and my husband never would. Of course, I can certainly help you with that." I pulled away from the curb.

Two agents slipped into the follow-up car. With a bit of guidance from the former first lady, I had no problem getting her and her daughter to their destination. I don't know whether the guys were disappointed or surprised, but it wasn't the first or the last time I had to be creative.

34

A Night at the Drive-In

WHEN PROTECTING youngsters like Caroline and John, I sometimes had to reach out of my job description, be creative, and laugh a little. After all, they were kids who wanted to live a normal life. They didn't like being in the public eye, and they didn't like having the Secret Service around.

When the Kennedy Center held its official grand opening in Washington, Mrs. Onassis decided at the last minute to go alone. I was left at the Kennedy Compound in Hyannis Port, Massachusetts, with John, Caroline, and a host of their cousins—all of them restless and bored. As the "pistol-packing nanny," a term coined by fellow agents, I offered an idea that might be fun. Sitting around the kitchen table in JFK's white-framed house nestled in the compound, I asked whether they had ever been to a drive-in. When I was a kid, it was one of my favorite things to do. They hadn't. So a night at the drive-in movie theater with homemade popcorn fit the bill.

While I popped the popcorn and John burned the butter, one of the other agents signaled that we had an intruder. I put down the popcorn, exited the house, and drew my weapon. We could see a woman walking backward up the hill, a large scarf wrapped around her head. Our eyes met, wondering who in the world this could be, and whether she was a threat to the children.

I called out, "Secret Service. Halt!"

The woman stopped, turned around, and smiled, and we recognized Rose Kennedy, the president's mother, walking toward us.

"Good evening, I'm Rose Kennedy," she informed us, somewhat unnecessarily at this point. "Just out for my evening walk, but the wind made it a bit more difficult. So I decided to take on the hill with my back to it."

We holstered our weapons and apologized. "Our mistake, ma'am," was all I could think to say.

"No apologies needed. I didn't mean to frighten you. I didn't want to muss my hair was all," she added.

I suppose that meant we were forgiven. Thank goodness we didn't arrest her. With the excitement over, we went back to popping popcorn.

When the snacks were ready, we piled the kids into our black sedan with siren and red lights. The kids brought their pillows. We were low on gas, so I pulled into the local Hyannis Port gas station to fill it up. After I paid, I got in the car and turned the key to start the engine. The car was unusually quiet.

Then all hell broke loose. They had pressed the buttons, turned the dials, and flipped the switches—turning on the windshield wipers, radio, siren, red lights, and who knows what else. At my expense, everyone, including the other agents in the follow-up car, thought it was funny. No good deed goes unpunished.

When we finally pulled up to the drive-in theater, the cousins announced that they wanted to "sneak in." I had an idea. I told them to get down on the floor in the back, pulled up to the ticket booth, held up six fingers, and asked for one ticket while I winked and smiled at the ticket taker. I paid for six tickets to see *Kelly's Heroes*, and they got to be "just kids" for a night. Everyone giggled a lot.

Unfortunately, they didn't get much of that in their well-watched lives. And truthfully, I enjoyed a night being a normal twenty-something myself.

35

Goodbyes

PEOPLE OFTEN ask me what Jacqueline Kennedy Onassis was really like. I was not there to know her well—I was there to protect her children. I know she was grateful for that. On some occasions she was approachable, other times not. In order to provide protection for the children, I needed to learn how to deal appropriately with that. She was always kind to me.

From what I witnessed, she was reserved, lovely, and an exceptional mother. The only thing she appeared to love as dearly as her children was their privacy. In some cases, I was privy to conversations between her and Caroline. Many books have been written about this remarkable woman, and it is not my intention to intrude into that space, but I don't believe she would mind my sharing a touching conversation that has been reported numerous times by her close friends.

One dreary, rainy day, I was driving Mrs. Onassis and Caroline to the Athens airport. They were discussing an upcoming event in honor of Caroline's uncle Robert at the eternal flame and burial site of President Kennedy. During the conversation, Caroline was quiet for a few minutes.

Then, talking about her father, she asked, "Why was he buried in Arlington National Cemetery? Why not Hyannis Port? He loved it there."

Mrs. Onassis smiled and quietly reminisced about a day when she and the president were returning to the White House from laying a wreath at the Tomb of the Unknown Soldier. "He told the Secret Service to stop the car and asked me to walk with him to this beautiful knoll in the midst of the Arlington National Cemetery overlooking Washington, DC. From that spot, you could see the Memorial Bridge, Lincoln Memorial, Reflecting Pool, White House, Washington Monument, and the Capitol," she told her daughter. "'If I could spend the rest of my life in one spot, it would be right here,' he told me."

I protected Caroline off and on for nearly two years. On my last day, we departed early in the morning for the airport. The sun reflected brightly on the white marble walls of the Athens Airport as I looked at her. She had just turned sixteen and was leaving for a summer in Spain. Children of a former president receive protection from the United States Secret Service only until they are sixteen. That day she was wearing her blue and white Diane von Furstenberg wraparound dress. It was her favorite; I had followed that dress with the same flat shoes many times.

As we walked to the plane, we laughed during short snippets of conversation about the antics of her summers in Greece and tennis camps in Austria. The time we outran the paparazzi and the night she got sick from too much ice cream in a contest downing chocolate sundaes. She won and spent much of the night in my room with me holding her head over the commode.

"Who will I borrow money from?" she chortled.

It was well known among the agents that the Kennedys rarely had cash on hand and we should have a little in our pockets. I always carried a couple of dollars. Caroline rarely did.

"What am I going to do without you?" she asked with a laugh.

I knew what she meant. It wasn't the fact that I had sworn to give my life to keep her alive and safe. She was concerned about her Coke and candy money. I will admit I was saddened by her departure. I was fond of her. Yes, she had purposely walked the wrong way down a one-way street with her friends to lose me, but I had enjoyed protecting her. Most of the time I did the best I could to be invisible, but when she swam too close to a stingray in Barbados or locked herself in an airplane bathroom, I was there. I rescued her from several difficult but not necessarily life-threatening situations across the world, and along the way I got to know her from afar. I was sure she would make her own mark in the world.

I was confident I did my job. I kept her safe, happy, and alive. We will never know what could have happened had agents not been there. In the end, nothing did, and that was the job of the United States Secret Service.

We said goodbye. After Caroline boarded the plane, like any mother, Jacqueline Bouvier Kennedy Onassis turned sadly toward the exit of the cavernous marble waiting area. Her head was covered in a dark scarf and she had her large sunglasses in place. Hiding tears, I would guess.

Mrs. Onassis walked alone in rhythm to the sound of wizened old Greek women dressed in black on their knees scrubbing the marble floors. I walked several paces behind her. Suddenly, she stopped and turned toward me.

"Thank you, Agent Clark," she said. "You have been a good friend to Caroline. I know she will miss you."

I still appreciate her kind words. That day, Caroline was a free woman. Without agents in tow, she could live beyond the glory and limitations of being the daughter of a former president of the United States. I was sure she would build her own legacy. Perhaps she would have a band of her own agents one day.

Then Mrs. Onassis spoke quietly about the fact that this was a special day for Caroline. "For the first time in her life, she is traveling alone," she said.

Today, she is over sixty years old and a successful woman and mother. Caroline is still classic and has certainly built her own legacy. I'll bet she is a talented photographer. She is published and has a liking for poetry. I was very proud when she filled the post as US ambassador to Japan. While we were not close, I hope I made her life a little better during the time our paths crossed.

John Kennedy Jr. and his governess, Marta, in the early 1970s.

The first time I met young John was at the Kennedy Compound in Hyannis Port. He pointed out his real live training plane in the backyard, a gift from the navy. It had no engine, but he loved to pretend to fly it!

US Ambassador Joseph and Rose Kennedy's home was the main building on the Kennedy Compound, which covered six acres of oceanfront property in Hyannis Port.

A signed picture
of former first lady
Jacqueline Kennedy
Onassis.

This is the view of Aristotle Onassis's private island of Scorpios from my post across the water in Nydri, Greece.

This time, guarding Caroline Kennedy (ninth from right) took me (third from right) underground into a salt mine tourist attraction near Salzburg, Austria.

Me (front) hanging out with ski instructors at the top of the mountain in Mayrhofen, Austria, getting ready to follow Caroline down the slopes.

Here I am (front and center) posing as an undercover camp counselor and leading the gang, including Caroline (fifth from right with long hair past her shoulders), on an afternoon hike.

In order to stay close by and protect Caroline (back row, far left), I had to blend in. On this day, I was a tennis instructor (back row, far right holding a tennis racket).

It was my job to keep the paparazzi at bay during Caroline's summer in Austria, but they still managed to come up with a photo or two of her having fun with her friends and cousins.

Caroline spielt Tennis in Tirol

Caroline Kennedy hat wieder ein Tennismat gewonnen. Kein Wunder, denn die hübsche Am rikanerin (Mitte), die zur Zeit in Mayrhofen (Tir Sportferien macht, wird von dem Wimbledon-Sieg Chuck McKinley trainiert. McKinley: „Sie ist d beste Schülerin, die ich je hatte." Caroline gab d Kompliment zurück: „Ein phantastischer Lehrer (Ausführlicher Bericht Seite 4.) Foto: AP

Mit Tennisschläger und Karate-Dame

Caroline in Mayrhofen: Sie trainiert eifrig, um ein Tennis-Champion zu werden

Auch wenn Caroline Tennis spielt: ihre Leibwächterin ist immer dabei

Von P. MILLARD und P. SCHMALZ

Mayrhofen, 1. Juli

Eine „Karate-Dame", die innerhalb weniger Sekunden jeden Mann „k.o." schlagen kann, ist Carolines neue „Gouvernante". Sie läßt die 15jährige Stieftochter von Ari Onassis (41) selbst auf dem Tennisplatz nicht allein. Denn sie gehört zur „Leibwache" der 15jährigen.

Caroline, die zur Zeit in dem amerikanischen Sportcamp von Mayrhofen (Tirol) für sechs Wochen Ferien macht, wird außerdem ständig von sechs „Gorillas" beobachtet.

Caroline möchte in ihren Ferien ein Tennis-Champion werden. Ihr Lehrer, der ehemalige Wimbledon-Sieger Bill Talbert zu BILD: „Das wird ihr auch noch schaffen. Sie ist jetzt viel besser."

Caroline darf in Mayrhofen aber nicht nur Tennis spielen. Gemeinsam mit 50 anderen Kindern aus amerikanischen Millionärsfamilien muß sie auch Deutsch und Französisch büffeln. Jacky Onassis (41) kann sich in die Wochen von den Fremdsprachen-Fortschritten ihrer Tochter selbst überzeugen. Denn gemeinsam mit „Ari" will sie zu einem Kurzurlaub nach Mayrhofen kommen. Der Großreeder möchte dort Skifahren lernen.

Caro
ist international

Caro trinkt man auch in Österreich und Holland, in Frankreich und in Belgien gern — und das rote Caro-Zeichen trifft man in Spanien und Portugal genauso wie in den USA und Australien ..... Denn moderne Menschen schätzen CARO!

As much as I loathed the tabloids, this day their headline worked to my advantage; calling me a "Karate Lady" may have scared off some of the other paparazzi.

On a rare day off, I got to be a tourist in Athens.

Special Agent John J. "Muggsy" O'Leary was one of my favorite partners. He is shown here during his early days as a Capitol Hill policeman protecting then-Senator John F. Kennedy, with whom he became fast friends. He gave me this picture as I was leaving the Kennedy children's detail.

With our appreciation and best wishes for a happy Christmas 1963
John F. Kennedy   Jacqueline Kennedy

Starting with President Calvin Coolidge in 1927, each sitting US president has given his White House staff and Secret Service detail an official presidential Christmas gift print. In 1963, the presidential Christmas gift print included a watercolor of the White House's Green Room. After completing the historic renovations, First Lady Jacqueline Kennedy commissioned artist Edward Lehman to create a series of watercolors of the restored interiors. Prints of the original watercolors were produced as Christmas gifts for the White House staff during the Kennedy administration. Tragically, the president was assassinated on November 22, 1963. Although official Christmas cards were never distributed that year, Mrs. Kennedy did give the Green Room prints to some staff and Secret Service after the president's death. Special Agent "Muggsy" O'Leary received one in 1963 and gave the historic print to me when I left the Kennedy children's protective detail in 1972.

Sweet assignment! This day, my undercover work included judging the summer camp's annual ice-cream eating contest. Caroline won first place!

A memorial service at Arlington National Cemetery on the anniversary of the death of Senator Robert F. Kennedy. It was a historic event when many of the Kennedys and younger Kennedy cousins were together, including Senator Robert Kennedy's wife, Ethel (center with crutches), her brother-in-law Senator Ted Kennedy (to Ethel's left), Caroline Kennedy (centered behind Ethel's right shoulder), and Maria Shriver (behind Ethel's left shoulder), among others. I am in the far right corner of the photo; I was protecting Caroline that day.

36

A Purse Fit for a State Dinner

MY ASSIGNMENTS were varied—a counterfeit investigation one day, then back to the White House for a protective assignment the next. One of my favorite protective assignments was with Princess Sofia of Spain. At the close of my first day with Princess Sofia, SAIC Jerry Parr pulled me aside and said he would like me to work the White House state dinner that evening.

"Normally the service just rents the guys a tux," he said. "Do you have something to wear?"

Did I have something to wear to a White House state dinner?

"Sure," I lied. I'd figure it out.

The lack of a dress wasn't going to keep me from this assignment! All I had was my Gamma Phi Beta sorority-pledge formal hanging in the back of my closet. The dress had a long, slim skirt nipped at the waist and a tight-fitting velvet bodice. Why I had brought it with me to Washington I do not know, but it was certainly fortuitous.

I jumped in my VW Bug and sped home to Georgetown. Bursting through the door, I said to my roommates, "I have to be back at the White House for a state dinner in forty-five minutes. Help!"

And help they did.

Ponce gingerly pulled the zipper past the small of my back. The dress still fit. A collective sigh of relief could be heard down Forty-Fourth Street.

Another roommate loaned me her wiglet. Women of a "certain age" most definitely remember wiglets, a small hairpiece in the crown of a formal hairdo. "Wiglets are a gorgeous way to give your hair more volume and a beautiful new thickness. Look great and feel confident," the advertisement said. With a mouth full of bobby pins, Ponce attached it and proclaimed, "It's perfect. You look great."

Imagine, I was about to depart for the White House to stand next to the Prince and Princess of Spain and the president and first lady of the United States of America.

I was ready, and I was going to make it to the state dinner on time. I doubt the agents covering the official visit of the Spanish royals had to worry about their waist size or a wiglet.

I stood in front of the girls looking and feeling good until I hoisted my bulky leather handbag over my shoulder with my .357 Magnum, handcuffs, badge, and commission book tucked inside.

The fashion police attacked.

"You can't possibly carry that to a state dinner," said Susan, the most sophisticated of my bevy of roommates. Panicked, I had to agree—but what to do with my gun? (On a side note: I've yet to meet a man who didn't ask me where I carried my service revolver. Men particularly love to ask that question. Sorry to disappoint you, fellas.)

None of the girls had a suitable evening bag that I could borrow. I had exactly thirty-nine minutes to buy an appropriate handbag and get to the White House. Ponce drove the car to the nearest store and double-parked.

With my badge in hand, I scanned Garfinckel's Department Store. A stout older woman dressed in a conservative black dress and sensible black shoes greeted me. Her glasses hung on a faux pearl necklace and moved in and out on her chest as she breathed. She appeared to be in charge.

"Agent Clark, US Secret Service. I need a black silk evening bag for my gun. Could you please help me?" I announced as I flashed my badge.

At first I thought she was going to call security. Here was a young woman wearing a formal gown and carrying a gun, claiming she had a fashion emergency that was of national significance. Instead, she quickly grabbed a handful of purses, escorted me to the dressing room, and held the curtains tight while I stuffed my gear into one of the dainty black numbers.

I have not intended this to serve as a handbook for Agent Fashion 101, but I have shared several "I don't have a thing to wear" stories about dilemmas I faced with clothing, purses, holsters, and handcuffs. I was, after all, a woman carrying a .357 Magnum revolver around the clock. From the very first letter I received from the training division outlining that I should wear white shorts and a T-shirt and provide my own "athletic supporter," it was clear they had no idea what women should wear during training or on duty. Nor did they pay much attention to it.

Dressing the part to work undercover as a hooker in New York or as a Vietnam War protester on the streets of Washington wasn't so tough, but to double as a guest at a state dinner at the White House was another story. I had no clothing allowance on my $8,500 a year salary. The men just rented a tux and turned in their bill. It was an ongoing challenge for all of us female agents in the early days.

The Forty-Fourth Street girls dropped me off at the East Wing entrance to the White House. The VW sputtered and lurched a bit as Ponce threw it into first gear and they waved out the back window. It was hardly one of the sleek limousine rides arranged for the invited guests arriving at the official entrance at the South Portico.

Making my way through the gate, I was thrilled to get a couple of nods and winks from my EPS buddies who were on duty. They had never seen me dressed like the dignitaries we were defending. I'm sure it was the wiglet that was catching their eye.

When I met with Assistant Special Agent in Charge Jerry Parr in the squad room, his instructions were simple: "Stay within a few feet of Her Royal Highness throughout the evening—no matter where she goes—until dinner begins. Then you will remain in the Red Room. The detail will remain right outside the door. We are never asked to dinner."

"How about the official arrival down the staircase from the private quarters with the president and Mrs. Nixon?" I asked.

"Take a position just to the right at the bottom of the stairs. Another agent will stand with you. Pick the princess up there," he stated and nodded to one of the handsome male agents wearing a tuxedo. At least I had a date.

There I stood at the White House, clutching my new Garfinckel's purse that housed more than lipstick and a cigarette, as the Marine Band, dressed in red military jackets, played songs from *My Fair Lady*.

My staircase perch gave me quite the view. As the band played, guests were ushered into a room filled with live cherry trees. Since it was not the time of year for them to bloom, the White House florist had glued fresh blossoms on the branches. Candles flickered, gowns glittered, important men in fancy dress uniforms and tuxedos offered their arms as escorts, and the aroma of the cherry trees made it an evening I will never forget.

On cue, the band's director tapped on the music stand, and the band stood and played "Hail to the Chief." President Richard Nixon, Mrs. Nixon, and Princess Sofia and Prince Juan Carlos of Spain descended the stairs. I was officially on duty. The guests were in awe. The princess was wearing a jeweled tiara and a dazzling necklace. Mrs. Nixon looked lovely in her pearls. I watched as the couples floated about the room making introductions, saying their hellos, and smiling with every new handshake. No one looked to be in danger, but I was on high alert. Being an agent means you're constantly on the lookout for something to go awry, even though careful preparation means there are very rarely any active threats.

During dinner, I sat on a red silk sofa in the Red Room. I thought to myself, I am in the same room where men gathered at the end of President Lincoln's first state dinner on March 28, 1861. President and Mrs. Lincoln were in this very room with friends when he received word that General Lee had surrendered at Appomattox on April 9, 1865. It was in this room that the president met with Congressmen George Ashmun and Schuyler Colfax just before he went to Ford's Theatre on April 14, 1865, and was assassinated. And here I was, a female US Secret Service special agent, waiting for the future queen of Spain to finish dinner with President Nixon. The historical significance of that night has always been a fond memory.

37

Regal Tourists

THE ROYAL couple spent several days in DC and the detail followed. One evening, we were assigned to an event at the Spanish Embassy. We arrived on time to the great hall of the magnificent marble Spanish Embassy building on Massachusetts Avenue. Standing below a huge chandelier and atop one of the largest oriental carpets I'd ever seen, second only to the one in the East Room of the White House, I was posted next to Princess Sofia in the reception line. I watched closely as invited guests moved toward her and she graciously greeted them. Even at the most formal functions, I was trained to keep my eyes on the guests' hands and eyes. I scanned the crowd looking for bulges in a waistband or unusual things that seemed out of place, such as someone wearing a heavy coat in summer or offering the princess a bouquet that hadn't been inspected.

Out of the corner of my watchful eye, something completely unexpected happened. An esteemed member of the president's cabinet walked directly toward me with his hand outstretched and his eyes fixed on me. His confident smile was that of a man ready to greet Her Royal Highness; instead he was on track to shake my little ol' hand.

This was not the kind of threat I'd been trained to eliminate. My mentors and instructors had told me that sometimes you just have to play it by ear. I boldly smiled back and extended my hand. Promptly guiding his outstretched hand to the royal on my right, I passed off his handshake.

"Your Highness," I quipped casually. "Of course you know Mr. Secretary."

"It's a pleasure," the princess cooed. We all did a fluid dance, everyone playing their part as we righted the mix-up. I might not have saved any lives that night, but I did what I could to keep American-Spanish relations intact.

In later years, when defending why women belonged in the Secret Service, my higher-ups would say there is no greater protection than the enemy confusing a female agent with the person we were protecting.

The magical White House evening came to an end and we escorted the Spanish royals across the street to the Blair House, where they were staying. All foreign dignitaries who were guests of the president stayed there. Another detail took over for the night shift. Special Agent in Charge Parr pulled me aside.

"You will be joining the detail on the remainder of the trip with stops in San Diego, Houston, and Florida. You better get home and pack," he ordered.

The next morning, I reported to the foreign dignitary command post at the White House and met the rest of the detail. It was early and the air was crisp. The city was just waking up. The sunrise peeked around the midsection of the Washington Monument. The waters of the Reflecting Pool and the Potomac did their job, adding to the magical color scheme. It was my favorite time to be on the South Grounds of the White House. The night shift handed the royal couple off to us at the south entrance.

We gathered our gear and walked across the manicured lawn through the shadow of Marine One, the presidential helicopter. In 1962, President Kennedy ordered a new paint scheme for presidential helicopters—green and white—with an American flag and the words "United States of America." The President's Sikorsky VH-3 also bore the presidential seal and was the first to be called "Marine One." In 1970, the Bell UH-1D became the official presidential helicopter. There are several such helicopters, but they are officially called Marine One only if the president is on board.

When we climbed aboard, the lumbering giant seemed ungainly until the pilot started the engines and the huge black rotary blades came to life. Lifting off, we and the royal couple sailed through Washington's restricted airspace to Andrews Air Force Base, where we boarded a plane frequently used as Air Force One, so called when the president was on board, the same as Marine One. That day, the sleek presidential aircraft answered to the call sign of tail number 2600 since it was on loan to the Princess and Prince of Spain. This was the same plane that returned the body of President Kennedy to Washington after he was assassinated in Dallas. As I buckled my seatbelt, I realized I was sitting in the section where President Lyndon B. Johnson had taken the oath of office, with Jacqueline Kennedy standing by his side.

During the rare and captivating experiences of being a Secret Service agent, it was this proximity to history—both momentous and tragic—that always brought me up short to remember the mission—to protect and serve.

In conversation, it became clear that both Princess Sofia and Prince Juan Carlos were very fond of our country and were anxious to see America. They walked about the cabin, gawking out the windows at the Mississippi River and the Rocky Mountains.

At one point, the princess sat with me and told me how much she loved America. As we approached California, the captain announced we were taking a special "dip" to get a better view of the Grand Canyon at sunset. It was spectacular! I doubt any other aircraft would have been allowed to do that.

For a few days, the royals stored their crowns in their bags and became regal tourists. We were not in charge of their schedule or unpredictable agenda. Yet it was my job to keep the princess safe, comfortable, and happy while she was a guest of the president of the United States.

As we arrived in San Diego, the princess whispered to me, hesitating a bit, "Do you think we could do a little shopping at a drugstore? I need to purchase some hypoallergenic makeup."

"Of course, Your Highness," I said and informed the State Department host.

The princess was always full of surprises. I don't think her host believed me. She had planned to take her to the high-end stores, but off we went to a local drugstore. Imagine a full motorcade, with Spanish flags adorning the fenders of the black stretch limo, a legion of motorcycles, and a string of black follow-up cars, pulling into the sprawling strip mall drugstore parking lot.

The agents, the State Department officials, and the princess made quite an impression on the local shoppers. Of course, I was the only one who knew where to take her. We found the makeup and went to the counter to pay. The princess pulled a large roll of one-hundred-dollar bills from her purse.

"Oh, honey," the gum-snapping girl behind the counter said. "You can't be throwing that kind of money around here. Somebody would kill you for that wad."

"Never mind," I said, pulling a twenty out of my purse. "I'll take care of it."

Obviously, the saleswoman didn't know who the princess and I were; the "fire power" surrounding the princess would have adequately protected her and her money. Princess Sofia thanked me, pushed the hundreds back in her purse, grabbed the paper bag, and the entourage left, complete with lights and sirens. When I looked back, the wide-eyed salesclerk, her mouth slightly agape, stood staring at us, chewing her gum more slowly.

After the official California visit, it was off to Houston. Shopping was again on the schedule. This time, Princess Sofia was eager to visit Neiman Marcus. To my surprise, she beelined to the costume jewelry counter.

Of course, anything from Neiman Marcus is beautiful. Apparently, all of the princess's regal jewels belonged to the state, but she purchased most of her everyday wear herself. "No one ever thinks a princess would wear costume jewelry. Some are real and some are not," she explained with a wink.

In moments such as this I didn't feel as far removed from those I was protecting. Sure, I wasn't pulling out hundreds, but what girl didn't love shopping at Neiman Marcus? No matter how different we are regarding wealth, status, or power, there are always commonalities between people. And in the lonely and thankless role of a Secret Service agent, it was nice to be reminded of that.

In 1971, I was on board Marine One (like the one pictured here), the presidential helicopter, with the Spanish royals as it took off en route to Andrews Air Force Base so they could travel to the West Coast for a whirlwind tour of the western United States.

Me with Special Agent Jerry Parr, the director of the Secret Service's Foreign Dignitary Division, aboard 2600 to protect the Spanish royals during their whirlwind tour of the western United States. When the president is on board, the plane is called Air Force One, and when he is not, it is called 2600.

Surrounded by agents (I am in the back, far right between the two men), the Prince and Princess of Spain make a casual tourist stop at a Spanish mission in Houston.

38

Rockets, Royalty, and Mr. Kissinger

MY ASSIGNMENT to protect Her Royal Highness Princess Sofia brought about a bonanza of experiences. Many fell into the category of "I never would have believed I would . . .": a state dinner at the White House; flying aboard the president's aircraft above the Grand Canyon; riding in a limousine armed to the teeth for a drugstore run; and shepherding a quick shopping trip to the "glamour go-to" store, Neiman Marcus, in Houston.

The last stop, however, was remarkable. I joined the detail when they visited Cape Kennedy on the Florida coast and was assigned a seat at NASA's Apollo 14 blastoff. The location is referred to as Cape Canaveral today, but in those days it was called Cape Kennedy.

As special guests of President Nixon, the royal couple was invited to join Vice President Spiro Agnew in the front row when NASA launched America's third spacecraft, Apollo 14, to the moon.

Today, space travel has become almost commonplace. Not in 1971. Astronauts were rock stars and travel to the moon was on the front page of all the newspapers. In a speech at Rice University given September 12, 1962, President Kennedy had thrown down the gauntlet that America should put a man on the moon:

> We choose to go to the moon. We choose to go to the moon in this decade and do the other things, not because they are easy, but

because they are hard, because that goal will serve to organize and measure the best of our energies and skills, because that challenge is one that we are willing to accept, one we are unwilling to postpone, and one which we intend to win, and the others, too. It is for these reasons that I regard the decision last year to shift our efforts in space from low to high gear as among the most important decisions that will be made during my incumbency in the office of the Presidency.

The fact that I was there has never lost its luster.

The Spanish entourage departed Houston aboard the presidential aircraft 2600 and flew to the Florida coast, arriving the night before the launch. The advance detail arranged for their protection at a VIP social reception and later at the site where the Saturn V SA-509 rocket was being prepared for the next day's launch. Then National Security Advisor Henry Kissinger and Vice President Spiro Agnew were scheduled to attend as well. I had been assigned to the vice president's detail in the past but had never seen the esteemed Mr. Kissinger. He would later become secretary of state.

Every bit the statesman, National Security Advisor Kissinger was a commanding presence, not unlike the other powerful men with whom I'd interacted. He was an important man and carried with him that aura of power. He wore his pants at his waist, tightly belted. Paunchy and fatherly, he wasn't handsome and was a tad bent over, but when he spoke it was with the confidence that anything he said would come to be.

At the VIP reception prior to the launch, I was told to stand post at the rear of the advisor's limousine while he and the royals were inside. The agent in charge told me to guard the limo's trunk with my life—literally. I didn't consider it one of my more intriguing assignments, but when I was told the cavernous trunk was filled with top-secret papers having to do with Kissinger's recent negotiations to end the Vietnam War, I stood a little taller.

Early in the evening, the advisor strode past me and gave me a quizzical look. "Who are you?" he asked slowly in his heavy German accent.

"Agent Clark, Mr. Kissinger," I responded.

"Secret Service Agent Clark?" he asked, appearing even more puzzled.

"Yes sir," I said, mustering a smile. "Special Agent Kathryn Clark."

Moving on a few paces, he turned and paused, and with a bit of a twinkle in his eye mumbled, "Why aren't you on my detail?"

Shrugging my shoulders, I took a deep breath and said, "I am not aware of any plans to assign me to your detail, Mr. Advisor."

"Oh," he said and moved on into the night. It was unusual to receive an informal comment from Mr. Kissinger. He rarely spoke to agents, and for a very brief moment, I was tickled he had acknowledged my existence. But the moment passed and I returned to my working-agent face and my job guarding the trunk.

An hour went by. With a crackle in my earpiece, the SAIC announced "Depart, depart . . . departing this location."

The guests were leaving the event and we were on the move to the launchpad. "Clark, Clark—roger," I acknowledged and took my place in the royals' follow-up car.

As we rolled into the entrance to Pad 39A at the Kennedy Space Center with sirens blaring, lights flashing, and a motorcycle escort accompanying us, huge floodlights washed the giant Apollo 14 launch vehicle, turning night into day. It was like driving onto the set of a Bond movie. Men wore white hard hats and jumpsuits with huge red letters spelling NASA across the back. Long black hoses and cables hung everywhere. Instructions and announcements came from a loudspeaker. There was a sense of urgency—and appropriately so. They were on a countdown to launch a rocket carrying astronauts Alan Shepard, Stuart Roosa, and Edgar Mitchell to the moon, propelling them on their quest for the history of the moon, the earth, and the solar system.

The royal couple and a few of us on the detail donned hard hats and were escorted to the elevator adjacent to the steaming rocket. The small black metal cage crept along the side of the Saturn V rocket with the letters USA in red, past an emblem of the American flag, to a platform adjacent to the rocket. At 363 feet, about the height of a thirty-six-story building, it was taller than the Statue of Liberty. I was awestruck. The Saturn V rocket took a dozen astronauts toward the moon from 1969 to 1972 and is considered one of the greatest engineering achievements in history.

Our NASA host explained that the samples of rock and soil they would retrieve from the landing site in or near the crater of Fra Mauro would be 4.5 billion years old.

"Tomorrow, during liftoff, the five enormous F-1 rockets under the first stage will generate seven and a half million pounds of thrust and burn five hundred pounds of fuel," he stated matter-of-factly. "That billowing cloud that looks like steam is a result of fueling the Saturn V's first stage with two hundred three thousand, four hundred gallons of kerosene fuel and three hundred eighteen thousand gallons of liquid oxygen."

"It's like riding aboard the world's largest Roman candle," quipped someone nearby.

"The journey will take the astronauts nearly a quarter of a million miles round trip," concluded our NASA host.

The invitation to such a historical event didn't have my name on it—I was there to protect the president's guests.

The next day, January 31, at 4:03 p.m., we watched NASA launch its third successful trip to the moon. At twenty-four years old, I sat next to astronaut Neil Armstrong, the first man to walk on the moon's surface, and listened as he gave the Prince of Spain his firsthand account of one of America's greatest achievements.

Mr. Armstrong was a very private man and gave few interviews. When the Prince of Spain asked how it felt to walk on the moon, he said simply, "Very small." To be in his presence made me feel small as well.

Mrs. Armstrong was the first woman to watch her husband walk on the moon. That doesn't exactly go down in the history books, but I heard her reference how much time she spent alone raising her family. She's an unsung American hero in my book. Too often the women supporting these "great" men are overlooked. I was, and remain, very impressed with Mrs. Armstrong's strength and determination.

The Armstrongs, the royal couple, and their detail sat in metal bleachers, a mere 1,600 yards from the launchpad. We could see the giant digital clock as its red numbers delivered the countdown to launch. Almost eight thousand other onlookers watched from a distance, and even more viewers lined the highways for miles, not to mention the millions watching on television.

Despite sporadic showers, the vice president didn't take his eyes off the launchpad as an orange flame blossomed beneath the huge rocket. When it roared into the sky, Mr. Agnew gripped the arm of Princess Sofia of Spain, seated on his left. I kept a keen eye out for potential threats to their security. That's why I was there. Yet I felt, smelled, and heard history that day. It was a remarkable memory in every way, something I will never forget.

After the blastoff, the detail moved our entourage into the NASA mission control room to watch huge black-and-white television screens broadcasting the progress of the flight. We stood alongside an army of men in dark pants, short-sleeved white shirts with pocket protectors, and short haircuts. Monitoring a myriad of small screens with an intensity I had never seen before and have not seen since, they looked as though they were collectively holding their breaths.

As a female agent, I blended in. In this instance, people assumed I was related to the princess or was her personal aide. Even CBS anchor Walter Cronkite appeared somewhat bemused and befuddled when he saw me. When the cameras first scanned the crowd, they focused on me. It did not go unnoticed by the princess; she laughed and nudged me. "They think you're me."

Cronkite had no idea who I was, as I am sure he had never seen a female agent before. The princess's reaction must have attracted the camera crew's attention, and they focused their feed on my protectee.

Across the country and the world, people huddled around TVs and watched and listened to Cronkite moderate the live coverage. He introduced the VIPs, including astronaut Neil Armstrong and the soon-to-be king and queen of Spain, as well as National Security Advisor Henry Kissinger and Vice President Spiro Agnew and his family.

Then he paused and said, "And to the right of the vice president is the director of NASA and . . ."

Then there was a very long pause. "But I am not sure who that unidentified woman is sitting behind the princess," he added.

At home in my parents' living room in Pleasant Grove, Utah, my sixty-five-year-old mother knew who I was. In those days, folks like my parents watched two things on television religiously—the Miss America Pageant and NASA space launches. I believe it was an extraordinary day for them. Rarely were they privy to the kinds of things I did on a daily basis, and to see it on a national broadcast was something they never would have expected.

39

The Theory of Relativity

SOMETIME AFTER my assignment protecting Caroline Kennedy ended, I encountered Mrs. Onassis walking alone on Fifth Avenue in New York. Her posture caught my eye. I'd recognize it anywhere.

My mind wandered back to my initial meeting with Mrs. Onassis. She was very reserved, and her voice was soft in a way that commanded greater attention than any shout could elicit.

As we neared each other, her eyes found mine and a look of warm recognition came over her. We spoke briefly. She asked what I had been doing since I left her children's detail.

"The usual," I laughed. "I've been assigned to several undercover counterfeit sting operations in between different protective assignments. I particularly enjoy the foreign dignitary details. The Princess of Spain was lovely. I travel a lot. In fact, I'm here in New York working Senator Kennedy's presidential campaign detail this weekend."

Mrs. Onassis exhaled and smiled graciously before responding in that sweeping whisper of a voice, "Agent Clark, you live such an interesting life."

We stood on the sidewalk in silence for a moment, two women in vastly different chapters of our lives, in positions we may never have imagined for ourselves, on paths that might never have crossed. Certainly there was no comparison, yet we both lived interesting lives.

Finally, I answered with a grin, "It's all relative, Ms. Onassis."

▫ ▪ ▪

I don't tell my story as a retrospective of the policy change inviting women into the Secret Service, but as an entertaining look back at a time that older women understand more clearly than younger folks, who have no idea how dismal the playing field was for us. Yes, I think the culture has changed in fifty years, but it takes time. No one said you can turn an ocean liner on a dime.

Why, some fifty years ago, did the Secret Service decide to bring women into the fold of one of the most elite, highly trained cadres of men to protect some of the most important places and people in the world? It's only speculation on my part, but my only historical reference is that I lived in the times when the higher-ups decided to do it and I was one of the five young women brought into the ranks to give it a try.

In the 1960s and 1970s, considered one of the most turbulent times in American history, the call for equal rights was on the table. Presidents like John F. Kennedy and Lyndon Johnson, and to some extent Richard Nixon, had listened. There was pressure from some women and push-back from others. The Equal Rights Amendment was essentially stiffed by women who believed equal rights weren't what they were cracked up to be. Yet some of the men in charge finally realized that women were not only wives and mothers, but a resource outside the home—and they had underestimated how ingenious we could be and how tough.

The "glass ceiling" is a metaphor to convey the undefined obstacles that women and minorities face in the workplace. I claim that the five of us did shoot holes in the glass ceiling of the Secret Service. Did we break it? Heavens, no. Did it crack a bit? Yes. Was it blown to bits? Definitely not.

Were we as women expected to defer to the men? Yes—not solely because they were men, but because they'd been there longer. Often simply tolerated? By some, yes. At times ridiculed? Probably—but for the most part I never heard it.

To my knowledge, college job recruiters rarely came calling or offering opportunities for women. Grad schools took a few women, the absolute best of the best, but enrollment certainly wasn't equal. I still applaud women who went on to obtain higher education. They were few and far between, but all amazing and committed. In my travels talking to women of the 1970s, I would say one out of three was first at something.

Yet as unlikely as it was, I was one of the few women who had the chance to rock the boat and test the waters, changing traditional values and the roles women were allowed to play. In the thick of it, I began to better understand the call for equality and the rallying cry that "well-behaved women rarely make history." By the time I left Washington, my politics had shifted a bit.

My story isn't just about the attitudes of an elite federal law-enforcement agency and the men and women who found themselves working shoulder to shoulder, not necessarily by choice but by federal mandate. They were about "the times that were a-changin'" and how we dealt with them each and every day.

I don't pretend to be a historian. My references to the history of that time are observations from my up-close and unique personal front-row vantage point. My story is just that—one of a lucky girl who fell into a rare job that was worth writing home about. I've done my best to send those letters your way and take you along for the ride. I hope you better understand the times and what I have called "Potomac Fever," and yes, I've told you what I wore and where I carried my service revolver because those were real challenges I had to deal with every day.

Should more women be hired to serve? I believe so. I believe today's women are even more prepared to serve in the mission of the Secret Service. Yet I do believe some jobs are better served by men and some by women. That's not to say I don't believe in equal opportunity.

Why hasn't the Secret Service hired more women? I'm not privy to that information. I think society is as guilty as the people who are in charge of how we live in it. In fifty years the number of female agents crept from five to five hundred. Today, 10 percent of Secret Service agents are women. It is apparent that changing human nature takes a very long time.

I received some insight into the service's commitment to seek and hire female officers and agents during a recent visit to Secret Service headquarters to tape a podcast about the early days. I was told that potential applicants for the job were weighing their options. Believe it or not, they say women today have options. They are being recruited to work in the "private or public sector, or with other agencies with a bit larger budget." Women have choices? Another wow.

The Secret Service understands that the reality surrounding today's recruitment climate revolves around the fact that the Secret Service must vie for the very same talent sought by the Federal Bureau of Investigation

(FBI) and Customs and Border Protection (CBP), which operate with vast budgets and seek many of the same candidates. Yet I encourage them to get the word out as best they can. I am frequently approached on college campuses by women asking how to throw their hat into the ring. I hope I will encourage more qualified women to apply.

My time in the United States Secret Service was short. Man or woman—if you are selected to serve as a special agent, you commit to more than a career, but a way of life. Personal choices and your life are not your own. As a woman, with perhaps more of those options to choose from, I chose a different path after a shorter period than I would have liked, but I don't regret a day I served and look back with pride and gratitude that I had the opportunity.

40

A New Protectee

I WAS ON a career track in the Secret Service, and that was exciting, interesting, and historic, but the journal of my personal life was rather dismal. I traveled constantly, oftentimes out of the country for months at a time. I was on call 24/7. I had no time to meet men, let alone date them. And yes, Mother, I carried a gun and handcuffs, which was sure to scare them to death. I was beginning to believe she was right.

Anna, my best friend and wonderful sister, decided to pitch in and find me a boyfriend. Anna was living with her husband, Curt Reemsnyder, a radiologist, in a lovely home in Corpus Christi. She had two kids and a carpool. On a visit to see her in Texas, she fixed me up with a dashing doctor friend of hers.

Cecil Childers was a psychiatrist and fifteen years my senior. Anna told him that I worked for the government. The rest we kept secret.

Cecil was tall and good looking, with salt-and-pepper gray hair and a sheepish grin. He had the kindest light blue eyes and asked more questions than he answered. He loved to sail and kept his boat at the Corpus Christi Yacht Club.

A special agent is always "on call," and I was required to carry my weapon with me at all times. When I boarded Cecil's thirty-foot sailboat, *Con Migo*, I stowed my worn blue flight bag containing my gun on the bunk below. It was a beautiful day, but the winds picked up, and the boat heeled. My .357 Magnum, handcuffs, six extra rounds of ammunition, badge, and commission book—not to mention my Revlon "Love That Red" lipstick—all rolled out. Cecil's eyes were big. Rather than being shocked, he was impressed. As he tells it, he's been saying "yes ma'am" to me ever since. Cecil didn't know much about what I did. I hesitated to go into too much detail, not knowing where the relationship was going, but he was intrigued.

We dated long distance for a year or so, meeting in Washington and Corpus Christi. Cecil was successful, fun, and often childlike in his enthusiasm for life. He seemed to like my independence and didn't mind that I was younger. I hoped that this relationship might work. We were both enthralled with one another.

Everyone called me Kathryn. In school I had been Kathy, a name that was so common that all the girls named Kathy had to be called by their last initial to distinguish them. I was known as Kathy C. When I graduated, I started going by Kathryn—a name that seemed more elegant to me. Cecil's pet name for me, however, was Kate, and he was the only one who called me that. I loved him for it. It is still a special name for me.

In the 1970s, unmarried people were just starting to move in with each other, and he asked me to move to Texas. "Not on my watch," I laughed. "I need a rock and a commitment before I leave my career."

I never figured he would come up with one, and I thought it would give me some time to keep the status quo in place. I continued seeing my handsome Texan whenever my schedule allowed, and I became more and more convinced he was "the one." I loved the romance, but I feared the reality of settling down and becoming a housewife.

Cecil called me regularly, or rather his very tenacious nurse, Gerry Heitkamp, did. I don't think doctors in those days knew how to dial the phone. Gerry could find me anywhere. Cecil would say, "Gerry, find Kate and get her on the line," and she would, no matter where in the world I was—Greece, Washington, or the White House.

One cold February day, I was at the Secret Service's outdoor shooting range in Beltsville, Maryland, shooting at man-sized targets with an Uzi submachine gun. The sound was deafening, with the chatter of multiple rounds of ammunition tearing through the paper felons. Empty clips fell to the cement as we discarded one clip and jammed in another. The rhythm was broken when an announcement came from the tower.

"Cease shooting! Make your weapons safe! Make your weapons safe! Agent Clark has an emergency phone call," announced the tower operator.

Eyes cut to me. My heart stopped. Something terrible must have happened to someone in my family. I feared the worst as I climbed up to the tower and took the call. Had my father had a heart attack? Was my mother ill? Or was it my sister? I was out of breath when the flustered instructor thrust the phone into my sweaty hand.

"Agent Clark," I said, expecting the worst.

It was Cecil. "Kate, Kate! I bought a ring! Will you marry me?" he asked.

"It's not a good time, Cecil," I whispered into the receiver. "I will have to get back to you on that."

Climbing down the tower, I took my place on the range and jammed in a clip. "Commence firing," was called over the bullhorn.

Cecil's unanswered question rang in my ears. I knew my life was going to change, and tears ran down my cheeks. He was ready to commit. I wasn't. I didn't know what to do.

Cecil brought my diamond engagement ring to Washington. It was a big one, and the reality of it all set in. I panicked. I applied for a transfer to the Houston Field Office with the hope of being closer to him in Corpus Christi, thinking that would give me an opportunity to be sure. The service wasn't very concerned about my love life, however, and I was transferred to the Los Angeles Field Office, where they needed a female agent.

With my ring packed away in its pretty red box and my transfer papers in my bag, I was completely perplexed at what to do. I sat on the grass in Lafayette Park across from the White House and picked the brains of a couple of hippie girls who were high enough to talk to me. Explaining my dilemma, I turned to them for advice.

They shook their dreadlocks and mumbled, "That's far out, man. What are you going to do?"

"I don't know," I cried.

One offered me a drag on her marijuana cigarette, but I declined.

I sent the ring back.

Cecil was patient. Considering that I had thrown down the gauntlet and demanded an engagement ring, which he had eagerly provided, and then I'd sent it back and taken the transfer to Los Angeles, Cecil was more than patient. He said little, but I knew I had hurt him terribly. Gerry didn't place any more phone calls.

I fell apart.

My sister Anna came to the rescue. She flew up from Texas, helped me pack my things into my car, and drove west with me. I skipped my going-away party. I just couldn't pull myself together enough to say goodbye. I cried as we crossed the Potomac River. We drove to Corpus Christi before heading to Los Angeles. I thought this would give me some time to pull myself together. Cecil wasn't there. He had gone ahead and taken his three sons to Washington, DC, for the visit we had planned before we broke up. Isn't that ironic? I was in Texas and he was in DC.

I arrived at the LA Field Office, where I had one agent friend, Sue Ann Baker, who had transferred from Washington to LA earlier that year. She offered me a room in her townhome in Fountain Valley, which was quite a distance from downtown Los Angeles. It seemed like all we did was drive. I greatly appreciated her kindness, and Sue Ann continues to be a good friend today.

The men in the LA office were receptive. I liked them a lot and made friends easily, but it wasn't Washington. I worked primarily counterfeit investigations and the protective detail when President Nixon was in residence at the "Western White House" at San Clemente.

Months went by, and I mulled over why I had chosen to send the ring back and move to Los Angeles. I missed Cecil terribly, but I knew there were valid reasons for being unsure. Marrying an older man would be complicated. Later his Alzheimer's proved that to be true. We were from different generations and backgrounds. I was a liberated woman, and he was a traditional fellow. He would want me to be a traditional wife—to be there each night when he came home. I loved having a career, yet I wanted children. I loved his sons, but I was scared about my role as stepmother to three young boys who already had a great mother. I loved him, but I wasn't sure I could keep up with his heart-charging Texas lifestyle. That was why it was so much fun to date him. It would be complicated. Texas, as they say, is like a whole other country.

Cecil had not called me in months, and I didn't blame him.

Then on July 1, 1973, Cecil called me on the West Coast and asked whether I would like to come to Texas for a Fourth of July party that weekend. I hadn't seen him in some time, and I missed him. "I would love to, but the president is coming to San Clemente, and I have to work,"

I confessed honestly.

"Oh, come on, Kate—can't you tell them you're sick?" he asked.

Obviously, the fact that I was scheduled to protect the president of the United States didn't seem important to him. "I'm sorry," I mumbled, and I truly was.

"Okay," he said flippantly. "I'll call you another time."

Within minutes, another agent walked into my office and told me I had the weekend off because the president had to attend a state funeral. I dialed Cecil immediately.

"I can come," I said excitedly. He cleared his throat, paused, and said, "Gee, I'm sorry, Kate. I have another date."

I was hurt, but I was in no position to be angry. Finally, I realized I was on thin ice with him, and I needed to make a decision—a big one— and fast. The next weekend I flew to Texas and surprised him. I think I proposed to him. He pulled the little red box out of his sock drawer and gave it back to me.

We were married in Carmel, California, on August 2, 1973, by a Lutheran minister, Father Grim, in a little wedding chapel at the Highlands Inn. Cecil and I always laughed about his name. In those days, you had to have a blood test to get a marriage license. Cecil's nurse, Gerry, liked me a lot and was ready for us to seal the deal. She actually gave her blood so he could get our license in Texas before he met me in California.

My parents, my sister, Anna, and my niece, Karen, came to our small wedding. My father walked me down the aisle of the tiny chapel overlooking the Pacific. We flew back to Utah for a party at my parents' home. Mother wanted Cecil and me to stay at the Hotel Utah in Salt Lake City, but it was a long drive, so we opted to bunk in a nicely remodeled chicken coop in the back of their peach orchard. Ironically, it was right behind the old fence where I had shot that very first can off the post.

Ever the jokesters, my brother-in-law, Curt, and my father rigged a cowbell under the bed attached to a rope through a hole in the wall. After midnight, my niece, Karen, and my nephew, Bruce, crept behind the coop, and amid giggles and shushing, rang the bell. So much for a sexy wedding night!

I had given the Secret Service thirty days' notice, so I went back to the Los Angeles Field Office to wrap up my career as a special agent. After one month, I turned in my gear.

My trusty little Volkswagen hadn't made the trip out West. I sold it in DC for one hundred dollars and bought a convertible from the Secret Service motor pool. The gleaming white-on-white Ford LTD was the personal car President Nixon had driven during his visits to Camp David, the presidential retreat outside Washington. It was a beauty and only a year old. If it was good enough for the president, it was good enough for me. I had taken out my first loan in my own name from the Treasury Department Credit Union and bought it for $2,900. Not only were women further up on the front line of equal opportunity, but credit was now within our grasp.

So I packed up my life in LA, put the top down on the Ford, turned up the radio, and headed south on I-405 toward the Mexican border and my new life in Corpus Christi. It was a gut-wrenching decision to end my career in the United States Secret Service. But that day, with the wind in my hair, I knew I was on my way to a new life with everything I had quietly longed for during my lonely nights in the service—a husband I loved, a built-in family—and I looked forward to having a son of my own, maybe even a dog.

Epilogue

WHEN I LEFT the service, I came back to Texas in a white convertible with the top down. I left a career I loved for a man I loved. I married him and inherited three stepsons, Cecil, Chris, and Jon, and had a son of my own, Clark. I reinvented myself multiple times as a television host, producer, writer, publisher, philanthropist, volunteer clown at our children's hospital, and now, speaker and author. Probably the most fun I had was driving a truck pulling an Airstream trailer thousands of miles across the country to see America with Cecil.

But it wasn't as easy as it sounds. It never is. There were heartbreaks along the way.

I spent the last ten years caring for my husband, who suffered from Alzheimer's disease. We survived one of the greatest natural disasters in recent times, Hurricane Harvey. Our home in Rockport, Texas, was at ground zero when the 150-mile-per-hour winds of the category 4 storm slammed ashore on our front porch. Recovery for the entire Gulf Coast has been an arduous journey. We were actually among the lucky ones.

When I left Colorado in 1969 in my baby-blue Volkswagen heading east to Washington, I thought I could have it all. I thought I could be a part of something important, excel at it, and eventually have a loving husband and a baby on my hip. But over the years I've come to believe that "no, Virginia—you can't have it all." At least you can't have it all at the same time. Marriage and motherhood in those days just didn't go hand in hand with a career. Today it is more the norm, but it still isn't easy.

I am grateful for my life. I am glad I can still blow out the candles on my cake. When I make a wish, I think to myself, "Been there, done that. Whatever's next, make it good!'

As they say in Texas, "Play the hand you're dealt." But you can't win if you don't play the game. When I think back to the day Mrs. Onassis told me I lived an interesting life or when the Greek widow shared her one nice coffee cup, I realize, relative or not, how fortunate I have been to have experienced some extraordinary moments and a life that has been a part of many important things to me.

I took the chance to do things that would scare most. I'm certainly not suggesting I wasn't scared; I'm simply saying I did it anyway.

Cecil passed away on the Fourth of July 2018, just shy of our forty-fifth wedding anniversary. I miss him terribly, yet I know he would frankly tell me, "Carry on, Kate."

In August 2019, I was invited to return to Washington, DC, to visit US Secret Service headquarters and witness firsthand how the agency has evolved—evolved in time, and by the cumulative actions and experiences of its personnel, whether one was there for a year or until retirement. I was told that professionally and personally, I, along with Phyllis Shantz, Sue Ann Baker, Holly Hufschmidt, and Laurie Anderson, and followed shortly by Denise Ferrenz, have "contributed to that foundation, which will forever expand with the contributions of others."

As I hear the sound of breaking glass in the background, I can say I'm proud to have been one of the "First Five."

The wedding day of Dr. Cecil A. Childers and me, Special Agent Kathryn Clark— August 2, 1973.

The entire Childers family during Christmas 2016 in Rockport, Texas (left to right): Adam Walton, "Sally, the dog," Clark, Cecil, Chris, Kathryn, "Ellie, the dog," Ben, Claire, "Molly, the dog," Jennifer, and Cecil III.

The "First Five" women hired by the US Secret Service in 1970 (left to right): Special Agents Laurie B. Anderson, Holly Hufschmidt, Kathryn (Clark) Childers, Sue Ann Baker, and Phyllis F. Shantz—pictured here in 2007.

Meeting up with Special Agent (retired) Clint Hill during his book and speaking tour.

Index

CPSIA information can be obtained
at www.ICGtesting.com
Printed in the USA
LVHW081239130322
713248LV00010B/10/J

9 781623 499167